Soul
Survivor

And this our life, exempt
from public haunt
Finds tongues in trees,
books in running brooks,
Sermons in stones,
and good in everything.

As You Like It
William Shakespeare

Paul Hawker

Soul Survivor

A Spiritual Quest
THROUGH
40 Days and 40 Nights of
Mountain Solitude

Northstone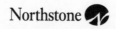

We acknowledge the financial support of the Government of Canada through the Book Publishing Industry Development Program for our publishing activities.

Permissions:
Excerpt from the Tararua Range Park Map, used by permission.

Adaptations of stories from *Unencumbered by Baggage*, and *One Minute Wisdom*, by Tony de Mello, used by permission.

Lines from:
"Irish Heartbeat" by Van Morrison, Music Publisher: Essential Music/PolyGram Music Publishing, used by permission.

"Give Me My Rapture" by Van Morrison, Music Publisher: Essential Music/PolyGram Music Publishing, used by permission.

"I'm Tired Joey Boy" by Van Morrison, Music Publisher: Essential Music/PolyGram Music Publishing, used by permission.

"Have I Told You Lately?" by Van Morrison, Music Publisher: Essential Music/PolyGram Music Publishing, used by permission.

"The Power of Your Love" by Geoff Bullock © 1992 Word Inc. US, used by permission.

Editors:
Michael Schwartzentruber and Dianne Greenslade
Cover design:
Margaret Kyle
Interior design:
Margaret Kyle and Rocio Launier
Consulting art director:
Robert MacDonald

Northstone Publishing Inc. is an employee-owned company, committed to caring for the environment and all creation. Northstone recycles, reuses and composts, and encourages readers to do the same. Resources are printed on recycled paper and more environmentally friendly groundwood papers (newsprint), whenever possible. The trees used are replaced through donations to the Scoutrees for Canada Program. Ten percent of all profit is donated to charitable organizations.

Published by
Northstone Publishing Inc.
Kelowna, British Columbia, Canada

Canadian Cataloguing in Publication Data
Paul Hawker, 1952–
Soul survivor
ISBN 1–896836–16–X
1. Hawker,Paul, 1952- 2. Solitude – Religious aspects. 3. Spiritual biography – New Zealand. I. Title.
BL73.H39A3 1998   291.4'47 C98-910016-2

Printing
9 8 7 6 5 4 3 2 1

Printed in Canada by
Transcontinental Printing Inc.
Peterborough, Ontario

*Dedicated to the
loving memory of
Paul Brandt
friend, mentor, and
guide for many years.*

Contents

Acknowledgments

My gratitude flows to all those who helped make my journey and this book possible.

First, to my family: Christine, Luke, Ben, and Toby Hawker who were willing to let me undertake the physical and mental risks of the trip.

To my friends, spiritual mentors and guides, who over the years helped ready me for the pilgrimage: my parents Beryl and Horace Hawker, Gordon Bennett, James K. Baxter, Te Wakaiti Community, Paul Brandt, Joanne and Jack Doherty, Sue and Michael Adams, Ted Woodley, Alan Robinson, Ian Robinson, Carlos Raimundo and Libby Checkley.

To the authors, poets and song writers who touched my soul with words to express the longings I felt: especially Van Morrison, Henri Nouwen, Gerard Hughes, and M. Scott Peck.

To Chris Peterson who offered to rescue me should the need arise. I am also additionally grateful to local radio operator Colin Coote, and the Mountain Safety Council of New Zealand for providing an emergency transmitter service.

In writing and rewriting the manuscript I am deeply indebted to Libby Checkley who, as well as correcting spelling, punctuation and grammar, kept me inspired, kept me honest, and kept me going. My gratitude also to my wife, Christine, for her highly accurate scrutinizing of and editing work on the final drafts and for bearing with me during the long writing process.

A special thanks to Dean Drayton and Tony Nancarrow who pursued a publisher for the draft manuscript. I am indebted also to Mike Schwartzentruber, my editor at Northstone, for his work in broadening the appeal of the text and for careful handling of the material so as not to disturb intended meanings. Thanks also to Margaret Kyle for the cover design.

The Spiritual Journey

Although most of us believe in some kind of supernatural deity, few of us suddenly "see the light." My spiritual journey, like that of most people, has been a gradual, gentle lifetime of discovery peppered with many experiences, much reading, and the occasional revelation. In searching for God and truth I have spent time with most of the major Western Christian denominations as well as been widely exposed to the ideas and thinking of other cultures and religions through literature and my work.

There is a problem, however, in describing spiritual experiences. I am well aware the word "God" comes with an enormous agenda and as I later explain, I find the word

*Don't search
for the truth,
Just let go your
opinions.*

Seng Tan 606 AD

*The search for what it
means to be spiritual
is the story, not just of
the decade but of the
century.*

William Hendricks

frustratingly inadequate, but for want of a better term I have continued to use it.

My wish is that you will find in here a relatively honest soul who would like to stand alongside you, to encourage you, but above all to join you as we all blunder along trying to make sense of our spiritual experiences.

Truth in religion is characterized by inclusivity and paradox. Falsity in religion can be detected by its one-sidedness and failure to integrate the whole.

M. Scott Peck

I am not a professional religious or cleric and have never held a paid position in any religious organization. For the last 18 years I have been a non-fiction television writer/ director. Apart from the odd charity video the vast majority of my work has been non-religious mainstream broadcast material. So in this regard mine is a religious voice that is seldom heard, a voice from the laity.

It would have been tempting to come down from the mountain and tell only of the insights gained, leaving out the failures, mistakes, conceit and bad behaviors. But I want to be open about what went on "up there" to show that I am no different from anyone else – that I too struggle with so much, and that each of our soul journeys is a lifetime affair with many stops, starts, hiccups, and branch lines along the way.

I claim to be no more or less than a spiritual pilgrim, a fellow traveler. I share this story of my experience of God in the hope that what touched me may also touch you, and for you to take what you need at this moment to help you along your own soul journey.

I trust you enjoy reading this as much as I did living it. Bless.

Once we become aware that we are on a journey – that we are all pilgrims – for the first time we can actually begin to cooperate consciously with God in the process.

M. Scott Peck

ONE

The Call Home

A chance conversation with a very old friend triggered a remarkable chain of events that still continues to unfold. I was telling him that as my two eldest sons had now left home I finally had the opportunity to do what I'd always wanted. The trouble being I couldn't remember what it was! It had been so long since I had been in charge of my destiny I felt as if I were drifting rudderless through life. I should have been happy and content. I thought I'd done everything I'd ever wanted to. In fact, life had turned out far better than I had expected. So why was I like this? Why so melancholy? Why plagued by this grief that had no reason?

*As if I were a river
The harsh age
changed my course,
Replaced one life with
another,
Flowing in a different
channel
And I do not recognise
my shores.*

Anna Akhmatova

"Sounds like you need a wilderness experience, mate: 40 days and 40 nights."

He watered a seed that had been lying dormant for a very long time. For years I'd had a deep desire to spend an extended period alone in the wilderness and now I somehow knew this was the time.

I was 43 and fully immersed in a busy television career – a privileged job that has given me access to an incredibly rich number of experiences: freedom to enter forbidden places, permission to probe private lives, opportunities to hear rarely divulged confidences, and the luxury of researching documentary topics to broadcast – what a colleague of mine refers to as the "definitive layperson's view."

Although no stranger to crisis, I wasn't in one at the time. Like many middle- class white males, I've had a fortuitous life with all the trappings of what society would deem success, including a great family. We laugh, cry, banter and bicker, and also celebrate, accept and enjoy each other. I think it's called love. Yet despite all this there was something missing, not quite right, a restlessness, a yearning. Without warning I'd be overcome by despair. Seemingly from nowhere, wave after wave of melancholy would wash over me and then recede, leav-

The first forty years of his life man explores the outer world. The next forty the inner.

Anon

ing me feeling alone, hollow, and a fraud. A part of me was missing, but I had no idea what it was. It was so deeply buried and long lost I could no longer identify it.

I announced to my wife, Christine, my intention to live 40 days and 40 nights on my own and she, used to my occasional life lurches, helped me buy the necessary alpine equipment, board a plane, and head off to New Zealand. There I planned to spend almost six weeks in solitude on a mountain that had touched me with its outrageous beauty 22 years before.

Back then I was overnighting in the small hut that nestles 100 meters or so below the summit of Arete. From where it was sited, I got an outstanding view – a sort of dress circle of mountains. But best of all, directly opposite the hut, about 700 meters away and at the same height, was a V-shaped pass. Looking directly through this pass I could see right out to the lowland hills and valleys stretching dozens of kilometers off into the distance. It gave the scene a natural picture frame that was quite extraordinary. I'd woken early in the morning, opened the hut door, and there stretched horizontally across the pass was a layer of beautiful pure white cloud with the golden sun starting to peak over the top. I was over-

It weeps in my heart...
This grief has no
reason.
Truly the worst trial
This not knowing why
With no love and
no hate
My heart has such
pain.

Arthur Rimbaud

A man travels the
world in search of
what he needs and
returns home
to find it.

George Moore

whelmed. It seemed put there just for me.

The grandeur of that moment has stayed with me forever – a kind of perpetual gentle haunting – not only the stunning beauty but also the unique timing. Had I risen a few minutes earlier or later I would have missed it. Being young I simply expected to experience many such events as my life progressed, and true I have seen many things of beauty. But events like this one, that I'd casually witnessed so long ago, didn't occur with anything like the frequency I'd expected. That morning's uncanny combination of physical events and my emotional state at the time served to forge what I can only describe as a spiritual union between nature, the divine, and me.

Footfalls echo in the memory
Down the passage
which we did not take
Towards the door we
never opened
Into the rose-garden.

T. S. Eliot

In the intervening years I have climbed many mountains – some real, some imaginary, many of my own making. But wherever I was, I searched. I didn't know what I was searching for, I just knew I hadn't found it. I looked for it in others, in achievement, in service, in adventure, in performance, in nature, in religion; and like a photograph slowly taking form as it gets washed back and forth in the developing tank, I gradually began to catch glimpses of it. Somehow I knew that returning to Arete was an essential part of the developing process.

Those in whom I confided my plans of sitting for so long alone on a mountain seemed to respect and understand my need to do so. It seemed to strike a deep chord in many and few felt the need to question why. Some thought it strange I was taking no camera, nothing to read, nothing to write on, that I was keeping no record of events; but as I pointed out, that would have made it a different exercise. Recording devices would give it a worldly purpose and through reading I'd allow the thoughts of others to influence me. I wanted this experience to be different, to go direct to the source. I wanted to go inside and listen to my inner voice and be directed by it – the voice I heard occasionally but didn't know all that well, a voice that at this stage I called God.

Although I'd occasionally connected with this God, all too often it had proved to be rather elusive. I wasn't completely sure if what I knew and experienced was real or just a construct of my mind. It wasn't so much a question of God's existence but of how to connect. What part of God was within me? What part was other? For years these questions had troubled me, gnawing away at my insides. A story I'd once heard illustrated my dilemma very well. It kept coming back to me again and again, softly tapping me on the shoulder.

No one is discontented at not being a king except a discrowned king... unhappiness almost invariably indicates the existence of a road not taken, a talent undeveloped, a self not recognised.

Blaise Pascal

You made us for Yourself, and our hearts are restless until they find their rest in You.

St. Augustine

There was once a young man who was seeking God. He'd heard of a great teacher who had helped many find their way so he sought an audience with him.

"You want to find God do you?" asked the teacher.

"Yes," replied the young man, "with all my heart, mind and soul."

At that the teacher raised an eyebrow and suggested they take a walk.

The young man was puzzled by this. Surely it would be easier if the teacher just told him how to find God? Instead they strolled along in silence.

After a while they came to a deep, slow moving river. The teacher walked into the river up to his waist and then motioned the young man to follow. This he did whereupon the teacher immediately seized him in a vice-like grip, plunging his head under the water. The young man struggled as hard as he could, but to no avail. Eventually, when it seemed almost certain he'd drown, the teacher released his grip. Gasping, retching and spluttering the young man took quite a few minutes to recover. Shocked, and by now quite afraid, he blurted out, "Why on earth did you do that! Are you trying to kill me?"

The teacher replied, "When you want God as much as you wanted to breathe air a few moments ago, that's when you'll find God." [1]

Did I want to know God that much? Was I prepared to risk all to find out – to put my neck on the line? The emptiness of not knowing the truth about a higher power had finally become too much. The first half of my life was over and I wasn't prepared to live the second half the same way – hedging my faith in "otherness," with worldly goods and achievements.

Nothing is better for a man than to be without anything, having no asceticism, no theory, no practice. When he is without everything, he is with everything.

Rainer Maria Rilke

I felt I had little to lose. I was a lost soul, directionless and confused. The unanswered questions had become as critical as life itself. It was crunch time. Time to discover what was and wasn't real, and to risk all in the process.

So in this search for God and self what did I plan to do? What about the boredom, loneliness, isolation and danger? Would I go mad spending so long alone? How would I cope? I didn't know the answers to any of these questions. I just knew I had to go. My only agenda was to turn up on day one, report for work if you like, and for once in my life let "The Boss" run the schedule.

---

[1] Adapted from a story by Anthony de Mello SJ

TWO

The Crucible

The range is extremely exposed to the northwest and the south, and has a reputation for high winds, fog and sudden weather changes. Rainfall varies from 5 – 7 meters a year, with the mountain tops cloud covered two days out of three. In winter, snow may lie above the tree-line for three to four months, and snow storms can be expected at high altitudes at any time of the year. Winter conditions on the high tops are harsh. Gale-force winds of subzero temperatures may blow for days or weeks on end.

Tararua Range Park Map, 1987

A journey is a person in itself; no two are alike, and all plans, safeguards, policing and coercion are fruitless. We find after years of struggle that we do not take a trip; a trip takes us.

John Steinbeck

Time engraves our faces with all the tears we have not shed.

Natalie Clifford Barney

It was late Autumn when I arrived in New Zealand. The mountain I was heading for is in the center of the Tararua range situated near the country's capital, Wellington. Known as "Windy Wellington," it is one of the windiest cities in the world. The reason it's so blustery is that the city is one of the first obstacles the "Roaring Forties" hit after their hell-bent journey halfway around the world. The gales are suddenly funnelled here through a 30 kilometer sea strait separating the North and South Islands. The city is sited near the shores of this strait in what must be one of the world's most effective natural wind tunnels. New Zealand's strongest ever wind gust of 283 kilometers per hour was recorded here only a short drive from the central business district. This was where I grew up, in the suburb furthest from the city but closest to the mountain ranges.

Since the tops of the range where I was now heading are the highest points near Wellington, they get a double dose of wind. At sea level there are usually trees and buildings to break up the gusts and create some shelter. On the mountain tops there is only alpine vegetation: moss, grass, lichens and rocks, with snow and ice in winter – no trees at all above 1000 meters. Consequently, anyone climbing on the summits and ridge tops is fully exposed to the howling gales.

As the mountains are close to the city, many people go in on fine days poorly prepared for the bad weather. Rescues are frequent and over 40 people have died there. Although not particularly high (only eight peaks are over 1500 meters) these mountains are not to be trifled with. If you wish to survive you must maintain a healthy respect for their unpredictable nature – a factor I'd experienced firsthand at a young and impressionable age.

I was 16 when invited by a friend to take a weekend trip over the highest mountain in the range, The Mitre (so named because when viewed from one side it looks like a Bishop's mitre). On Saturday we climbed in cloudy but calm conditions and I wondered what all the fuss was about. Dire warnings of death by exposure or being blown off the ridge seemed little more than horror stories told to scare beginners like me. Although my friend had been quite insistent I take a pair of windproof overtrousers, I was convinced I could have done without them – they were rather heavy. Like most teenage boys, having no experience to the contrary, I believed I was invincible.

Sunday was totally different. As we began the return trip the wind was gusty,

Every soul is a melody which needs renewing.
Stéphane Mallarmé

As you pass from the tender years of youth into harsh and embittered manhood, make sure you take with you on your journey all the human emotions! Don't leave them on the road, for you will not pick them up afterwards!

Nickolai Vasilyevich Gogol

increasing steadily over the next few hours. Buffeted this way and that we were blown over many times, but the lasting image I have is that of my friend bent over and walking about ten meters in front of me. Without warning, a sudden gust plucked him off the ground, heavy pack and all, and momentarily suspended him in midair. Then as the gust changed direction he was slammed back into the ground a few meters further on. Luckily it wasn't precipitous for had it been so he might have been badly injured or worse. I was suddenly very scared.

For the rest of the trip we crawled along the lee side of the ridge leading up to the summit. That day I gained a profound respect for the elements. In the future I paid particular attention to forecasts, trying to avoid the exposed tops when gales were due and always carrying storm gear regardless of what the weather looked like. This and other life-threatening incidents in the mountains had a profound impact on me from which I made up some life rules. Attributing my survival to good management rather than good luck, and elated by my perceived success and physical prowess, I set out to conquer these mountains.

Rarely using tracks, we increased our

bush-craft skills, learning to successfully navigate where others would lose their way. In so doing we gradually became more competent and confident of our own abilities. I accumulated experiences that convinced me the best way to operate was to rely on my own strength, native cunning, and will power. I had become conditioned to be a great survivor.

These skills and attitudes I carried over into my world outside the mountains. Majoring in survival tactics I was perfectly attuned to look for and react to outside events: a fine day – head for the mountain tops; a rainy day – make the most of the river valleys. Find out what people want and give it to them; when the boss says "jump" you ask "how high sir?"; give them the answer they want to hear, not what you really think. Just as I viewed the weather, I tended to act and react to the events that blew my way.

It served me well financially, but took a terrible toll on my soul, for I had sold the right to be who I really was. I believed survival for me and my family depended on my efforts, my ability to navigate uncharted territory, my performance and my strength to climb a mountain, be it made of rock or manmade. I even believed survival for myself as a husband and father depended on

The human heart refuses to believe in a universe without a purpose.

Immanuel Kant

One's real life is often the life that one does not lead.

Oscar Wilde

my performance. In all things I was afraid that if I let up and stopped paddling for a minute I'd lose it all. That I constantly had to try harder, that people only liked me because of what I could do for them.

I believed that held true whether providing them with food, effort, love, entertaining company, supplying a film they liked, or simply being a "good" person. I thought if people really knew what I was like I'd quickly be deserted and destitute. I simply didn't believe I would ever be accepted for who I was and I was too afraid to risk finding out.

One's own self is well hidden from one's own self; of all mines of treasure, one's own is the last to be dug up.

Friedrich Nietzsche

With no deep inner core I was a candle in the wind. At this stage I had no words for my malaise but for years two songs kept going round and round in my head: The Eagles' *Lying Eyes* and The Platters' *The Great Pretender.* They seemed to reach me somehow.

My malaise came out as restlessness and discontent – feelings I alleviated by seeking interesting films to make, places to visit and challenges to pursue. Sure, they were fun, stimulating and satisfying, but as each new event passed into my suitcase of memories, satisfaction became increasingly elusive. I ached to have my motivations come from within me. Not just to "survive" outside events, but to live, really live, the life I was born to lead, to be that which has always been inside me. The me I didn't even know.

I was envious of those special people I'd met whose aura of peace I was instinctively drawn to, those who had a deep inner strength welling up from inside them. Men and women who were open and vulnerable yet at the same time incredibly strong. They had such strength within them that you knew no matter how much bullying, guilt, fear and shame they suffered; no matter how much money was offered; no matter how important the status of the person they were dealing with; no matter how they were ill treated or manipulated they would remain the same. People who knew who they were, where they stood and why they were alive. I had met them in all walks of life: Jim the poet, Paul the manager, Steve the fishing-tackle shop proprietor, Bridget the nun, John the advertiser, Indira the politician, Roy the painter, Tony the doctor, Desmond the Bishop. Their occupation, class, sex or religion seemed to be of little consequence. What characterized them all was that they weren't afraid.

They knew fear but didn't respond to it the way I and most others did. I ached to

We are so accustomed to wearing a disguise before others that eventually we are unable to recognise ourselves.

François, Duc de la Rochefoucauld

There are some people who, when you meet them, exude an almost tangible peace and gentleness.

Peter Vardy

have what they had – to move out of the house of fear I was living in and to reclaim my lost soul capital. This then was my prayer for me as I prepared to enter the hills armed with prayers from others.[1]

[1]My soul journey had an incredible support network – kind thoughts, pledges of support and a powerful line-up of precious people who sent up requests on my behalf.

THREE

Day One

The day dawned clear – always a bonus in New Zealand! An old and dear friend had taken the day off work to drive me to the road end and we arrived there midmorning. As I struggled to get my backpack on, we joked about the Himalayan porters that were bound to turn up any minute. A few hugs and some kind words later, I was off into the rainforest that covered the foothills of the mountains.

As I waved good-bye, I soberly considered this might be my last interaction with another human for almost six weeks, perhaps forever. For I had gone to great lengths to ensure I would be undisturbed. I insisted no one was to come looking for me regard-

*Whenever I prepare
for a journey I prepare
as though for death.
Should I never return,
all is in order.*

Katherine Mansfield

less of how long it was since they had heard from me. Although I had an emergency radio, I could expect no rescue should I become lost, fall or injure myself and be unable to rig the cumbersome 40-meter aerial.

I had done all the practical things to prepare for the journey. There was nothing more to do. This was it, the day I was to turn up. From this point on, my inner and outer journey was going to be guided not by pre-set destinations or timetables, nor by my level of fitness or tenacity, but by the inner voice. At this stage, I claimed to be open to whatever would be called, that I would obey the will of The Master, even if that meant never setting foot on the mountain or coming down before the 40 days were up. I had a lot to learn, mostly about the rules I still had in my head but was quite unaware of, a set of rules so deeply entrenched that dislodging them would take superhuman forces.

However, all this was secondary to the delight I was experiencing, free and alone in the rainforest on a stunningly fine day. As I walked along the rough track that burrowed its way through mighty cathedrals of centuries old trees, I caught occasional glimpses of the mountain tops, clear, strong and bold, their grey cold lines standing erect and proud on the skyline.

*I like trees because
they seem more
resigned to the way
they have to live than
other things do.*

Willa Cather

The streams I crossed tumbled, giggled and jostled their way, coursing downhill as would children released from school after a hot sticky day in class, bouncing and splashing their way to freedom. Drops captured momentarily in the light glistened and shone before falling back again into the turmoil.

The forest's mass of lush verdant growth was staggering, but what catapulted my visual senses into overdrive were the greens; everything was green, a thousand shades of green! Leaves, needles, stalks, trunks, mosses and ferns almost overpowering in their flamboyance. An explosion of emerald.

I buried my hot sweaty head into one stream, feeling the ice cold sharpness on my lips, sucking its life-giving moisture. I rolled the pure virginal freshness of unpolluted water around in my mouth, before allowing the precious fluid to course down my throat. Nature's finest champagne, untouched by metal pipe or concrete reservoir, as free and untainted as the day it came into creation. Yes!

Sheer joy at last, totally alone with nature – an unlashing of my heart's cry to be here. Years of busy-ness had parched my soul, shrivelling it up and now, now it was being replenished! Today I felt free. I was free to decide when to go this way or that and

Nature is the living, visible garment of God.
Johann Wolfgang von Goethe

Man on his way to Silence, stops to hear and see.
Alice Meynell

for how long. Whether I stood, walked, crawled or cried was my decision alone and would affect no other person. I could stay here for over a month if I chose to, rain, hail or shine. For snail-like, I had everything I needed on my back to survive. No questions to answer, no demands to be met, no routines to keep, appearances to keep up, people to let down or disciplines to adhere to.

We need the faith to go a path untrod, the power to be alone and vote with God.

Edward Markham

The only other times I've come anywhere near experiencing this freedom is alone on long international flights. No matter what goes wrong at the office, no matter what family crisis appears, for a few hours I cannot be involved. I have permission to be out of contact, out of action. When I return, no one is going to chastise or accuse me of being selfish or unapproachable or inconsiderate. Because "I'm flying," everyone understands I'm isolated and uncontactable. Sheer bliss!

The solitude I sought in the mountains (and relished on my international flights) is a part of me. A deep desire to be alone, to reclaim and re-examine that which I was before I put on the adult clothes of spouse, father, employee and citizen: to be at one with my spiritual self, without having to defend or protect it against those who belittle or don't understand it, to be guided by

God in me. It had been a long, long time since I had been alone, truly alone like this. I savored every second.

This was how my inner journey was going. However, my outer journey had developed some interesting practical problems that I now had to contend with. My backpack was very heavy. Subzero storm clothing, tent, repair kits, first-aid kit, sleeping bag, air mattress, torch, clothes, stove, plus fuel and food[1] for nearly six weeks meant I was carrying well over 40 kilos. As a young man I would have found this "a bit of a challenge" but as an unfit overweight, over 40-year-old, it was a bit of a shock. Walking was fine; the problem was getting down or up.

To sit down for a rest I had to find a tree or a bank, prop myself on it, and ease out of the shoulder straps, leaving the backpack balancing precariously. Standing up was the reverse of this, but where no bank was available I had to roll onto all fours, go into a crouch, and then slowly lever myself up.

It is easier to sail many thousand miles through cold and storm and cannibals, in a government ship, with five hundred men and boys to assist one, than it is to explore the private sea, the Atlantic and Pacific Ocean of one's being alone...

Henry David Thoreau

---

[1] I had been persuaded out of the idea of completely fasting, because to deliberately starve in the conditions I was going into could be quite dangerous. I didn't want to have supplies dropped, as that would destroy my solitude, so I opted to carry my food. I took what I considered to be the minimum for survival. Daily rations were two cups of milk (powdered), some rolled oats, a dehydrated meal, rice, a few nuts, some soup, plus a multi-vitamin and vitamin C tablet. Daily calories 1150. I could choose when and where to eat this, so fasting for a couple of weeks or so was still an option. The total weight of food at this stage came to 11 kilos.

*In actual life every
great enterprise begins
with and takes its first
forward step in faith.*

August Wilhelm von
Schlegel

*Beginnings are apt to
be shadowy.*

Rachel Carson

Floundering around on the forest floor I must have looked like a beached whale! I was just too heavy to stand up unassisted.

This being the case the inner voice's calls to stop and admire the scenery weren't always well received! Any deviation from a measured walk soon turned into a major exercise. Within a few hours the exertion was becoming quite painful. The backpack harness dug into my shoulders and back; and my feet, unaccustomed to over 120 kilos pressing down on them, had splayed out into the creases of my boots and were developing major blisters.

But there was a more immediate problem. The track I was on sidled along about 50 meters above the river gorge. Classed as an "easy" walk, the path meandered in and out of the many side streams that ran down into the river. The last few streams I'd crossed had been quite difficult for me to climb out of, as my overloaded legs were being attacked by severe cramps. I'd stop and rest for ten minutes or so, then go another 100 meters before the cramp set in again. Each rest produced less and less cramp-free time, so much so that I was now able to walk only a few meters after each spell. It was coming on to dark and I began to realize that things might not be as rosy as I had been making out. There was a hut about an hour's walk away, but in my condition it may as well have been on the other side of the moon. As for camping, I was still in the gorge and there were no areas flat enough for a tent site.

I couldn't believe it! Here was the great outdoor adventurer, solitude hero, forced to crawl along like Quasimodo. Racked with pain, each step was an agony. I couldn't care less for the beauty that was around me now – all I wanted was relief from this torment! However, I was too pig-headed to ask for divine help just yet. I pretended I was doing just fine and didn't need any celestial interference, thanks very much. No, you can rescue me up on the mountain, save it until then. Eventually it got too painful, even for my pride, and I asked for help.

I'd brought a small packet of dried beef jerky with the intention of using it only in a serious emergency. To my mind this cramp business didn't really class as a life-threatening event. It being my first day, I had no idea of what hazards or dangers lay ahead, so I was reluctant to eat it now as it might mean the difference between life and death later on. But something had to be done. I took the risk and ate some. Jerky's very salty and salt is a great antidote to cramp, so

God is subtle, but he is not malicious.

Albert Einstein

If Jesus, the healer, taught us anything, he taught us that the way to salvation lies through vulnerability.

M. Scott Peck

within ten minutes of eating I was able to walk again, if somewhat stiffly.

Right on dusk I arrived at the hut which to my great relief was unoccupied. The effects of the beef jerky were wearing off and I was about done in. I didn't have the energy to pitch a tent in the dark and to do so would also have meant using my torch and running down some of the precious batteries that were supposed to last 40 nights.

I'd just taken my backpack off when two other climbers walked in! So much for solitude! I was angry. Not with them, they had as much right to be there as I did, but at the circumstances that had broken my solitude. I mumbled something to them, shoved my backpack back on and headed out the door to a campsite I'd noticed a few hundred meters up river. They must have wondered why I was in such a hurry to go somewhere at that time of night. (In the mountains you sometimes meet some strange people!) After arriving at the campsite and unpacking I discovered to my dismay that in my rush to leave the hut I'd left my hat behind! It was a crucial piece of equipment, without it I'd be compromising my safety on the open mountain tops.

A very contrite, weary, and thoroughly beaten soul-traveler walked back into the hut later that evening and rolled out his sleeping bag. It had just gotten too hard to fight anymore. My rules about what was and wasn't to be had been broken. My body had collapsed on me, I couldn't as I had claimed "camp anywhere." I'd eaten a large portion of my emergency rations, had called in a favor from the Big I Am, and had my solitude broken almost as soon as it had started! I felt foolish and ashamed, and exceedingly glad I had no one with me to see my collapse.

Where did I get these rules from? Whose rules was I supposed to be playing by here? Who had decided what was and wasn't to be? Who had put in place the criteria I was living by? I had a lot to learn.

A man's first care should be to avoid the reproaches of his own heart.

Joseph Addison

FOUR

Solitude

It's amazing what a night's sleep can do. From being quite depressed the previous evening, in the morning I was positively chirpy. I reasoned that since yesterday was only day one, if I extended my time to 41 days I'd still have 40 without human contact. Besides, hadn't I had a glorious time yesterday in the rainforest?

Getting up early, I spent a few hours just being still in the forest, standing in the clearings, smelling the dew, listening to the bird life and the gentle, soothing, rumbling, tumbling of the river. Man, nature, and the divine spending time with each other – sounds idyllic? Well almost. The problem was I couldn't concentrate on anything for

The longest journey is the journey inward.

Dag Hammarskjöld

*In solitude, where we
are least alone.*

Lord Byron

*I throw myself down
in my chamber, and I
call in, and invite
God, and his Angels
thither, and when they
are there, I neglect
God and his Angels,
for the noise
of a fly,
for the rattling
of a coach,
for the whining
of a door.*

John Donne

very long, in fact about a nanosecond, before my mind was off somewhere else.

I've read about monks who spend years trying to totally empty their minds of all thoughts and images. It's counted as a tremendous achievement, when for five or six seconds they have nothing, absolutely nothing in their heads. It clears the way for God to speak to them. Well, God wasn't even going to get a look in on my mind the rate I was going! What a mere mortal like me had when I finally stopped and stood still was "monkey mind." I called mine "bees." My head continually buzzed with supposition, conjecture, conversation rehearsals, script line tryouts, plans, worst case scenarios – a seething mass of overlapping tumbling thoughts, leaping all over the place, each new notion clamoring for attention with none leading anywhere in particular. (I mean no insult to bees; they are far more intelligent creatures than this suggests.)

Here I was, surrounded by peace, beauty and tranquillity, free to enjoy the eternal presence with no demands to do anything; yet inside my head a fireworks display of unconnected random thoughts was shooting off in all directions! I'd stare at the tumbling river, the frond of a plant, a shaft of sunlight cutting through the tree canopy, or a bird on the wing and then realize with a start that I wasn't looking at anything. My eyes saw while my mind wandered.

I knew the meditation techniques I could apply to rid myself of this, but I didn't want to use them and end up "achieving" the goal of a blank mind. My time in here was too precious for that. Besides, I'd been there and done that and I wasn't all that convinced it would get me any closer to the heavenly realms. I figured if the claims about God were accurate, I didn't need to jump through any hoops. God would decide when and where to meet me, if at all. It was entirely the Creator's call. If I meditated in some trance like state and had a vision of the Divine, I could too easily claim I had created it, and then I wouldn't have God, just my version of God. No, I wanted the real thing even if it meant being buzzed to death in the process.

Returning to the hut midmorning, I was relieved to discover the two climbers had gone. I sat in the sun for a while and then took my time packing up. I was just about to go out the door when I heard voices! I couldn't believe it! What solitude? This time it was two hunters. At this rate I'd have to stay in for months to get a clear 40 days!

If God wants us to do a thing, He should make his wishes sufficiently clear. Sensible people will wait till He has done this before paying much attention to Him.

Samuel Butler

The spirit's foe in man has not been simplicity, but sophistication.

George Santayana

The problem of so many people being around was partly due to being only a few hours walk from the road end and partly because there was a holiday weekend coming up. As I was going further into the mountains and well away from the road end, there would be fewer people. Nevertheless, I resolved to find a quiet spot to camp and so avoid any further interruptions. I set off with the best of intentions but within an hour I realized that it didn't matter what my mind wanted to do, my body wasn't going to cooperate. My feet had blistered so deeply, every step felt as if red-hot nails were being poked into my soles. Walking was agony. I was forced to slow down and stop. Whatever agenda I had to climb my mountain was now abandoned. I hobbled onto an island in the riverbed and there found the campsite of my dreams.

It was perfect. Like a scene from Bambi, it had beautiful birch trees, a pixie glen of soft moss and grass with lovely views onto the river. My low-line tent blended in so well it was almost impossible to spot. Well off the track, I wouldn't be seen if anyone traveled past, which was just as well since the fear of being discovered again was almost making me paranoid. On either side of the island and across the river, the hill slopes boasted some

Alone, even doing nothing, you do not waste your time. You do, almost always, in company. No encounter with yourself can be altogether sterile: Something necessarily emerges, even if only the hope of some day meeting yourself again.

E. M. Cioran

spectacularly tall trees – gentle giants of the forest. It was so tranquil and calm.

The condition of my feet meant I'd have to stay put for quite a few days. It was quite a relief to know this. I spent the rest of the day sitting still and let the silence touch me. As the river gently bubbled away over the rapids and the shadows began to fall, I welcomed my first night in the wilderness totally alone. I felt no apprehension and had no fears for my safety. Away from all other humans, there was no one who could do me any harm. I relished the isolation, and surrounded by nature's perfect cocoon I slept soundly.

Over the next few days I was taught how to listen and respond to my inner voice.[1] Knowing that I wouldn't be disturbed, I sat perfectly still and allowed the sun to reach out and touch me, full, warm, and soft on my face. Like a flower, I'd slightly tilt my head so as to better drink in the full essence of this life force, almost tasting the growth it promised. Slowly I'd sink down as each part of me let go and relax into an awareness that I, too, was a part of the natural cycle.

The only sounds were the bubbling of

Peace is when time doesn't matter when it passes by.
Maria Schell

[1] The discernment process used to distinguish what was and wasn't from the spiritual world is explained in Appendix 1.

the river and closer by, the hum of flies and bees. Occasionally the stillness would be broken by a bird call or the gentle rustling of leaves caressed by an isolated breath of wind just passing by. I looked at, and felt, the serenity around me, soaked up the un-ruffled tranquillity and relaxed into a peace that knew no boundaries. Waiting and lis-tening like this, occasionally I'd be invited to go for a

Wander and wonder

nowhere in particular, just to enjoy what I came across. Sitting or standing, I'd just look and watch for hours. Placing my face centimeters away from the tiny lichens and mosses that grew on dead and dying trees, I saw that each one was a universe on its own – minute fronds, millimeter-high grasses, and fractionally higher "trees." Each a perfect microcosm of its bigger cousins, a mini-forest, each area its own ecosystem. So much unknown activity going on within a few square centimeters – fascinating.

So how did I know where to go? Why stop in a particular place? Sometimes it was the sheer beauty that attracted me, I couldn't help but stop and watch. Some-times it was the bird life; sometimes I'd go to move and a song would pop in my head.

God, I can push the grass apart And lay my finger on Thy heart.

Edna St. Vincent Millay

I believe a leaf of grass is no less than the journey-work of the stars.

Walt Whitman

Oh won't you stay?
Stay a while with your own one . . . .
the world is so cold
Don't care nothing for your soul
That you share
With your own one.
© Van Morrison

Why was I so keen on moving? I had days, weeks, over a month to do nothing except be here. So where was I going? It was just habit. I sought a change of scenery to stop me from being bored. So I'd stay a while with "my own one" to see what would happen.

Often something would occur that I might have missed had I moved on: a shaft of sunshine highlighting a leaf in a particular way, a thought in my head that movement may have blocked. Often it was like watching time-lapse film: light would rest a while on a patch of the forest floor and slowly move centimeter by centimeter as the world turned. Once while staring mesmerized into the depths of a pool, an insect fell into the water right in front of me. It struggled to escape until a tiny bird flew down right beside me and picked it up. I resisted the temptation to name the bird, ascribe it to a particular species or analyze

In solitude we discover that our life is not a possession to be defended, but a gift to be shared. In solitude we become aware that our worth is not the same as our usefulness.

Henri Nouwen

*A solitude is the
audience-chamber
of God.*

Walter Savage Landor

*Most men pursue
pleasure with such
breathless haste that
they hurry past it.*

Søren Kierkegaard

its behavior – I just enjoyed the privilege of being so close to an event that in my normal, busy rush mode I would never see.

I avoided time-filling activities such as building a better campsite or exploring the area. These would distract me from my real purpose – to wait on God's calls. Even walks were off the agenda, as the steady pace of walking is as an effective time-measuring device as any clock. I sensed time-filling activities such as these would turn the whole exercise into an endurance test and crowd out the inner voice. I'd had 43 years of that already, I was determined this was going to be different. I only wanted to do what The Master ordered.

It was so hard at first, as it was my usual habit to constantly invent mental destinations and goals. I had to regularly remind myself not to pick a bluff, tree, river boulder or outcrop and then head there ignoring all else along the way. For such had been my tendency – so hell-bent on setting and achieving goals I regularly missed what was right in front of me, what I already had. So now I paused, stopped and stared at leaves, trees and scenes for minutes, sometimes hours. I found through this that I began to celebrate and enjoy the journey rather than the destination.

As I settled in and took the time to pause and reflect and let the wonder of it all touch me, I was unaware of the subtle and gentle process that was under way. I was being given a crash course in learning how to slow down, to get in tune with the gentle rhythms of grace – part of the preparation necessary to make me physically, emotionally, and spiritually fit for the journey ahead. At the time I didn't know this was what I was involved in, I just enjoyed it. It was wonderful.

It is in this solitude that we discover that being is more important than having, and that we are worth more than the result of our efforts.

Henri Nouwen

FIVE

The Valley

As the days of solitude rolled by I sensed that the hours spent watching, waiting, and being still were more than a nature observation exercise, that somehow through my stillness I was learning something. I hadn't watched life like this since I was a child and as I settled into being rather than doing I began to realize I was encountering a rare experience for an adult Western human – a completely unscheduled life.

Normally my head is like an electronic airport flight arrival and departure board – as soon as a plane lands or takes off, the letters and numbers flip over to reveal a new schedule. So it is for me with my self-assigned routines. While completing the task

The logic of worldly success rests on a fallacy: the strange error that our perfection depends on the thoughts and opinions and applause of other men!

Thomas Merton

at hand, my mind rosters ahead, flipping and rescheduling all the other events of my life into a new order.

In work mode, it's bookings to be made, contacts to chase up, ideas to formulate, crews to arrange, accounts to process, phone calls to make, appointments to keep, traffic to avoid. In my home life, it's partner to spend time with; kids to take places; cars to maintain; chores to do; friends to call; television programs I just have to see; newspapers, books and magazines to read.

Remember that as a teenager you are at the last stage in your life when you will be happy to hear that the phone is for you.

Fran Lebowitz

Every now and then, just like the airport concourse, an urgent page penetrates the public address system in my head: dog whining – needs a walk; train late – child needs picking up from station; phone rings – a decision has to be made. The list goes on and on. I rarely get completely unscheduled moments. When they do occur, they're often brought on by crises such as cancelled appointments, missed flights or traffic jams, so I fret or worry them away.

I'd measure success by what I'd done. Time was money. If I wasn't "doing" I'd soon start to feel guilty. I'd have nothing accomplished, nothing to show for the time I'd "wasted." When asked what I'd done all day, I'd have no answer – a crime that could only be redressed by redoubling my efforts to make up for "lost time" and achieve what should have been done. My diary was a log of activities, a balance sheet to see whether my achievements were in profit or loss. It was relentless, never ceasing. Even on holiday I was bound to an agenda treadmill that exhorted me to exhaustion.

Children don't schedule things and perhaps this is why they have such an amazing sense of peace and wonder. If left alone they take the time to look and see, really see. Their only priority is what's immediately in front of them.

Now, for the first time in probably 30 years, I was truly engaged in what was right in front of me, experiencing life as a child might. I was captivated by the natural pleasures of what unfolded before me, rather than what I could make happen through my own activities. Perhaps this was life as it was really meant to be! Unscheduled bliss. It felt wonderful! Seldom bored, I watched and waited allowing the great silence to overcome me.

I enjoyed my Own One as a child would a good father, as if God was my closest confidant or a wise loving older uncle. Pointing out stuff, asking "Why?" I would lose interest in the answers, try to listen, and then ask, "What's next? What am I waiting for here?"

The national distrust of the contemplative temperament arises less from an innate Philistinism than from a suspicion of anything that cannot be counted, stuffed, framed or mounted over the fireplace in the den.

Lewis H. Lapham

And eventually I'd get answered.

Wait. Give it time. When it's ready.

And then I'd be moved on again. Often I'd be invited to

Look at the water.

Watch the rapids.

Linger a while.

Enjoy this.

Never before had I ever had such an uninterrupted opportunity to be alone and fully engaged with my Own One. I was with my Master, fully aware, fully alive, at home in the divine garden, feeling The Creator's pleasure in being with me every moment of the day.

It wasn't all serenity and bliss. I was constantly plagued with doubts. Was I hearing right? Is this really God's voice? Maybe I'm just making it up? I was rarely 100 percent sure, but went ahead anyway. If it wasn't from the right source, I trusted I'd be guided back onto the right path. I was really an amateur in all this and I was bound to make mistakes, stumble, and get it wrong.

That is what faith is: God perceived by the heart, not by the reason.

Blaise Pascal

First I had to learn to respond – to hear, trust, and obey. As well as wandering and wondering, I was asked to rest, sleep, and do exercises. These consisted of touching my toes and deep knee bends. At first I could hardly even manage half-a-dozen of them, but gradually more came. This exercise program was different from any I'd ever done before. This wasn't a "no pain no gain" activity. Instead of straining and pumping, my Master was accommodating. No predetermined times to exercise, or how many activities to do, just

Exercise... that's enough now; it is finished.

I had a personal trainer who was intimately concerned I didn't overdo it, damage myself, or become discouraged. Progress was measured not by fitness levels but by my Coach's guidance and approval. It was gentle.

I also prayed, not on my knees, just wherever I stood or sat. I'd made a commitment to spend time petitioning for four special people to be healed, but I was also regularly asked to

Pray for the lost.

This became a discovery journey on its own.

The first dozen or so times I appealed generally. It didn't mean much to me and I'm sure it meant even less to God. It was a quick-fix prayer, one I might gush out as an afterthought squeezed in between my other more important daily activities, like earning money, watching TV, and reading books. It didn't measure up out here in the wilderness

There are thoughts which are prayers. There are moments when, whatever the posture of the body, the soul is on its knees.

Victor Hugo

where I had all the time in the world. Besides, it soon got quite boring. I'm sure God was bored by it too, but as I was continually asked to do it, I struggled on.

It still seemed wrong, so I expanded it and started talking about people I knew. Initially this was far more interesting, but as I named folk a problem developed. I didn't know who was or wasn't "lost," what did "lost" mean anyway? In fact it was quite an arrogance on my part to name those "found" and those "lost." How did I know? Only God knows that. So I changed, asking that they be touched in some way, that God in them and around them would be revealed in ways that they might understand.

This seemed to apply regardless of what particular spiritual season a person might be in. This way I could leave soul matters in the best of hands, not mine. I'd also add a wish prayer for them:

"Please release him from fear."

"Let her know love, true love. "

"Convince her that she doesn't have to perform to be accepted and loved."

"Soften his heart so that he can receive the love others so desperately want to give him."

I came up with these wish prayers by asking myself, "If I was God, what would I

Faith begins as an experiment and ends as an experience.

Anon

What we know of other people Is only our memory of the moments During which we knew them.

T. S. Eliot

most desire for this person?" Viewed this way, it seemed to strike directly at their real, heart issues, touching my heart too, for I began to see them as an all-loving God might.

Over the days I thought about these people and asked for love to be given them. I gradually realized how much they had touched me and had been a part of me, be it ever so briefly or over long periods of time – work colleagues, relatives, family, associates, mates, friends, churchgoers, neighbors, people I only knew by sight, authors, acquaintances, companions, school chums, teachers, shop assistants, bosses. As I named each one, it gradually began to dawn on me that if I wanted these people to be loved perhaps they might want me to be loved as well? I knew so many of them had touched me, taken risks for me, even loved me. What a strange and beautiful thing! In asking God to be there for them, I received insight into how loved I was, something I'd previously been quite unaware of.

I am loved so profusely by so many. As a friend used to tell me when I was periodically racked with the crippling pain of self-doubt, "You're lovable and capable, how come you're the only one who doesn't know that?"

Today I knew.

It is only with the heart that one can see rightly; what is essential is invisible to the eye.

Antoine de Saint-Exupéry

The beginning of love is to let those we love be perfectly themselves, and not to twist them to fit our own image. Otherwise we love only the reflection of ourselves we find in them.

Thomas Merton

SIX

Trees

Day six, another fine one. Incredibly, still no rain. Was this the day I would move on, closer to the mountain? As the days ticked over I'd frequently ask, "Is it time to go?" Sometimes I'd get a definite

Not yet!

and other times I'd get no reply at all – nothing. This was often the response to many of my questions. Nothing. I guessed the silence might mean my question was inappropriate or not ready to be answered, but really I just didn't know. I put this one, along with all the others, in the "to be revealed" basket and waited for further instructions.

One thing I had learned was, when I heard nothing, I should do nothing. Some-

There are three answers to prayer: Yes, no, and wait a while. It must be recognised that no is an answer.

Ruth Stafford Peale

times doing nothing is exactly the right thing to do, but it's a response I am quite unaccustomed to. I usually see activity and productivity as a measure of my and others' worth, so to do nothing is to be worthless. I certainly needed a lot of educating in this area.

Wander and wonder.

I slowly meandered up the hillside toward a massive tree I'd admired many times. This was a Rimu, a giant of this particular rainforest, at least 40 meters high and over two meters through. I gazed upward in awe of its longevity. There is something incredibly powerful about centuries old, long-term natural survivors like these. I love touching and hugging them, pressing my ear to their trunks and whispering, "You beauty, you wonderful thing you" and then a parting comment, "Best of luck, tree." This last one I'd learned from my father.

A very conservative man, he had no truck with any way-out ideas like talking to trees, but he loved gardening. One evening, as I watched him planting out vegetable seedlings, he momentarily forgot I was there and engaged in what was obviously a very familiar routine to him. Breaking off his humming, he'd murmur to each plant as he tenderly tucked it into bed. "There you go…

hum hum... best of luck, lettuce... hum hum... best of luck, cabbage... best of luck, caulie..." Each one had its individual blessing in the same way that he blessed me when he kissed and tucked me into bed at night. If those plants felt anything like I did when I was put to bed, they couldn't help but grow!

I passed on this blessing to the giant and continued to gaze up into its lofty heights, savoring the wonder of it all. How many storms had it weathered? How many humans had touched it? (Very few, if any, as it was well off the track.) Measured alongside its time scale and size, how insignificant I must seem. As I circled around its base, I was struck by the way its buttressed roots and sinewed gables soared skyward, triggering the same sense of greatness I've sometimes experienced in grand cathedrals. Here in the rainforest I felt the same sanctity as I would in a consecrated church. I was in a holy place built perfectly by the master architect. As it was a Sunday, it seemed appropriate to honor the moment. Deep in the half light of the forest I worshiped in this sacred site.

After 20 minutes or so I noticed the once bright sunshine was beginning to darken. Suddenly, incredibly, I broke the sanctity of

Why are there trees I never walk under but large and melodious thoughts descend upon me?

Walt Whitman

The "kingdom of Heaven" is a condition of the heart – not something that comes "upon the earth" or "after death."

Friedrich Nietzsche

the moment and rushed to the edge of the forest in time to see a band of drizzle heading down the river valley toward me. I dashed back down and across the river to my campsite on the island.

What on earth was I doing? I could hardly believe my behavior. Inside was this gentle pleading. . .

Remain, stay. It will be all right.

Where are you going?

Why are you leaving ?

I'd been seriously derailed by a few spots of rain and the other voice...

Hurry up and get the tent in before it gets wet, you know how heavy a wet tent is to carry. Do it now! The rain is coming – look, can't you see it's going to pour any minute? Don't worry about breaking the sacred moment, you can always come back here again and I won't mind, I'm a loving and forgiving God. Quick, don't delay – do it now before it's too late.

I ran and in a semi-panic, took down the tent and hurriedly packed my backpack.

As it out turned, it didn't even rain on my campsite! My tent would have stayed dry. The rain, for some mysterious reason, stopped a few hundred meters up river. Humbled, I went back to the tree and tried

The bitter and the sweet come from the outside, the hard from within, from one's own efforts.

Albert Einstein

to pick up where I'd left off, but it was now very different. The sense of sanctity had gone. It was just another big tree in the forest. I'm sure I was forgiven – The Creator had no issue with picking it up again – the problem was I couldn't forgive myself. My rules said, "You shouldn't make mistakes like that. You're bad to abandon your God after all that's been done for you. Haven't you learned anything?" I was so hard on myself, angry at what I had missed out on and how I'd destroyed the moment. With more allegations of wrongdoing, the accuser had had a field day; and there was more to come.

A few hours later I left my campsite and headed up river. I don't know whether I was asked, or whether I just decided. Anyway I left.

After five days it was good to be moving on again. My blisters had healed sufficiently so as to no longer cause pain and I enjoyed walking over the grey round river boulders and the occasional broad grassy river flats. The red deer had cropped the grass so short that the flats looked like well-groomed picnic areas.

My backpack was much lighter as I had left five kilos of rice behind. I hadn't been eating nearly as much as I thought I would, so I calculated I could easily shed some ex-

Uncontrolled, the hunger and thirst after God may become an obstacle, cutting off the soul from what it desires. If a man would travel far along the mystic road, he must learn to desire God intensely but in stillness, passively and yet with all his heart and mind and strength.

Aldous Huxley

cess food. Energy-wise, this now meant I would get around 850 calories a day, below the daily healthy minimum, but I felt that as I was in such good hands this wouldn't be a problem. I regretted not bringing more rolled oats with me; unlike rice, they can be eaten raw and I quite enjoyed them.

Continuing on upriver, I was passing by an attractive waterfall when the old 1960s' pop song *Stay* popped into my head. I paused, gave the waterfall a few seconds' glance, and travelled on. The song kept playing. I knew it referred to the waterfall, I knew I was supposed to stop, sit down and rest a while to view it and most probably have something revealed to me. I knew I wasn't doing what was required, but I was in "go mode." I had decided I wanted to get somewhere. I thought I'd gain more satisfaction from achieving the goal of arriving than from sitting and contemplating.

God gives us the nuts, but he doesn't crack them.

German proverb

I soon came to a small clearing where a one-person, cableway swing bridge was strung across the river. This was a junction of three routes and as there was a hut nearby there was a possibility I might come across someone. Five days had passed since my encounter with the hunters, but I told myself that seeing as it was late Sunday afternoon logically there was little chance of anyone being in the hut. The inner voice was warning me to be careful, but just as I had done back by the waterfall, I ignored it.

I then heard voices, real voices, other people! Desperately I turned around and tried to run back down the way I'd come. With my full backpack I must have looked totally ridiculous. They called out a friendly greeting. Damn! I'd been seen. I had been sprung. Sheepishly I told them I was trying to avoid people, and they, quite puzzled by this weirdo, obligingly moved on. I was devastated.

Later, I read in the hut logbook that they and one other party were the only ones to have passed through that week. If I had stayed just a few minutes by the waterfall I would have missed them completely! Now I could only hope to have 34 days solitude. I felt cheated, the purity of my wilderness experience had been sullied. All that time spent camping wasted, how could I ever retrieve it? Did I have to start again?

Who gave you these rules?
Who said it had to be this way?
Who says it's spoiled?
Whose criteria are you using?
Why have you made these conclusions?
It is nowhere near finished yet.

We cannot get to God under our own steam. We must allow God to do the directing.

M. Scott Peck

I prefer the folly of enthusiasm to the indifference of wisdom.

Antatole France

Considerably sobered by the day's events and with much of the fight gone out of me, I realised I'd been forced into accepting things as they were, rather than how I would like them to be. That night I didn't even feel too bad about making a call on the mountain radio to let the outside world know I was all right. (As previously arranged with Mountain Safety, I placed these calls at approximately weekly intervals.) I also decided to stay in the hut rather than camp. I now felt I had little left to lose so why try harder?

It rained quite a bit over the next few nights so I was very glad to be indoors next to a warm fire on a dry mattress. There was also a half-kilo of fresh rolled oats in the hut.

Too long a sacrifice Can make a stone of the heart.

W. B. Yeats

Thank you. Being less virtuous certainly made life easier!

Despite my "screw ups" I still had a deep sense that I was "on track," that my "mistakes" were all part of the exercise, that there was no pre-set right or wrong path, I just had to keep going forward. That night as I lay on my bunk thinking, I felt something had changed. I couldn't name it, but like Gulliver in Lilliput, tied down by hundreds of tiny threads, I felt as if a few strings had come loose and I could move about more freely.

SEVEN

Enlightenment

Day seven.

Fetch wood and carry water.

I laughed. So this was it, the passage to enlightenment! There wasn't much water to carry and I didn't have to go far to get it. Surprisingly, collecting wood was a lot of fun. I had unlimited time to range quite far afield to find the dead and fallen branches. I built up quite a supply of firewood for myself and future hut inhabitants. I did it well too, not skimping on the dry kindling and breaking up the big pieces so that whoever arrived next might enjoy a hearty fire. When I'm not under pressure to finish, chores such as these are so wonderfully fulfilling; doing them well somehow feeds my soul. It's in-

The man is happiest who lives from day to day and asks no more, garnering the simple goodness of a life.

Euripides

credibly satisfying, like the time I picked up the rice.

One morning back on my island campsite, I was reorganizing my food. As I picked up a bag of rice, it left behind a trail of white grains. Overnight a mouse had chewed a large hole in the plastic bag. Thinking little of it I just brushed some leaves over the spilled rice with my foot. Later on that day I was asked to pick the rice up.

In character, in manners, in style, in all things, the supreme excellence is simplicity.

Henry Wadsworth Longfellow

It was my choice how to do it and, having more than enough time, I decided to do it grain by grain. It amazed me what a pleasure this task turned out to be. Because there was no deadline to complete the job, I could take my time and make a good job of it, one I could be proud of. I rarely had this luxury at home where usually the criteria was to finish as much work as possible in the time available.

My fingers soon tired from pinching the small grains so I used the pliers on my Leatherman® pocketknife. If I wasn't careful, the pressure from the pliers would break the grain, which meant instead of picking up one grain I'd have three. Even so, it wasn't a chore. As I picked up each grain and carefully put it in my cup it became almost meditative. This indeed was an entirely different way of operating.

If I am faithful to the duties of the present, God will provide for the future.

Gregory T. Bedell

How is the rice picked up?
One grain at a time.
How is the rice picked up?
One grain at a time.

As I wasn't wearing a watch I can't recall how long it took, but judging by my muscle discomfort I estimate around 40 minutes. When I put the last grain in the cup I was almost disappointed the task was over.

Wash the rice.

This I did. Many times I rinsed it carefully from cup to plate and back to cup again. If any grains spilled I picked them up and rewashed them. The rice was becoming almost sacred.

Eat the rice.

Before doing so, I considered the tiny grains. I realized that because I had rescued each one from the forest floor and carefully washed it, I cared so much more. By investing time, care and attention into them, they were now a part of me – especially since I hadn't had to do it, it had been my choice. As I nibbled away on the raw starchy grains, I was grateful to them for a very timely lesson. Perhaps if I treated other objects or people in the same way, how much more would I love and care for them? How much more would I gain if I took the time to care about myself? Maybe it is in loving others

In solitude we are in the presence of mere matter (even the sky, the stars, the moon, trees in blossom), things of less value (perhaps) than a human spirit. Its value lies in the greater possibility of attention. If we could be attentive to the same degree in the presence of a human being . . .

Simone Weil

like this that we gain the most for ourselves?

I was brought back to the present moment by an interesting natural phenomenon unfolding in front of me. There had been quite a dump of rain overnight and now as I sat beside the river I watched the water turn from crystal clear to muddy within the space of a few seconds. It also began to rise; I could see it creeping up a centimeter or so every few minutes. Rocks that were exposed to the air soon became immersed.

Far from idleness being the root of all evil, it is rather the only true good.

Søren Kierkegaard

As I watched the river rise, I also noticed that the rays of sunshine penetrating the forest canopy were striking patches of wet green moss beneath the trees, releasing a slow moving, gently swirling mist. The delicate dewdrops on the tiny moss fronds sparkled when touched by such a "heat ray." I took off my boots and snuggled my bare feet into the warmed moss. Delicious! How I savored this warmth for the fresh gift it was. During the morning I followed the sun's movement to each newly warmed patch of moss, wriggling my toes into it, reveling in the moment of heat until my weight pressed the deeper, colder layers of moisture up into the soles of my feet. It reminded me of a story I'd once read where some poor children were growing up on a dairy farm during the 1930s depression. They used to warm their bare feet on cold frosty mornings by stepping into the newly dropped cow pats. Today I knew the pleasure they felt.

I stayed in and around the hut for the next two days, led to exercise, wander, rest, consider, watch, experience, meditate, pray and obey. In so doing I began to build up a precious reservoir of confidence that I would comply to the inner voice's calls. This in turn allowed me to go easier on myself and trust that, when asked, I would obey and that it was okay to make a mistake or two.

I decided that the next day, day eight, I'd start to climb regardless of the weather. I had asked regularly and often for a fine clear day. There was no voice, no song in my head, no invitation, but in the same way I was drawn to go there in the first place, I knew it was time, time to start climbing the mountain.

In solitude we can slowly unmask the illusion of our possessiveness and discover in the centre of our own self that we are not what we can conquer, but what is given to us.

Henri Nouwen

EIGHT

The Mountain

I used to climb by toughing it out, ignoring the thirst, the tiredness and the pain, only dropping down to rest when totally exhausted. I would constantly push myself harder and harder to get fitter, to get there quicker, to reach the top while it was still clear so that I wouldn't miss out on a view.

Great things are done when men and mountains meet. This is not done by jostling in the street.

William Blake

This trip was to be different. I wanted to abandon the "crash-through, I'm-not-going-to-let-it-beat-me," sheer will power methods of the past and instead try to apply the gentle rhythms of grace: to submit to a higher power; to let that power call my steps, when to rest, when to move. I wasn't sure how it would turn out. I was still an infant in learning these rhythms and the temptation to go for it and try harder would be strong.

I'd certainly need all the help I could get. A week on minimal food rations had put a bit of lead in my saddle, as had the backpack still heavily laden with a month's fuel and food.

So, early in the morning I set off uphill with this question-and-answer session rhythmically going around in my head:

How is rice picked up?

One grain at a time.

How is the mountain climbed?

Half a step at a time.

As I slowly ascended, the thick sturdy tall trees successively gave way to more stunted beech trees, each clad in luxurious green fur coats of moss. These, too, gradually decreased in size as I continued upward until finally, around midday, I reached the last band of tough, scrubby leatherwood bushes that signaled the tree line was close.

As I emerged above the tree line the wind was bitterly cold, but the storm clouds that had been there most of the morning had now lifted and it was clear enough to navigate along my intended route. This was a huge relief as I had not been this way before and I was unsure I'd be able to find my way in fog. What perfect timing!

> *The strength and happiness of a man consists in finding out the way in which God is going, and going in that way, too.*
>
> Henry Ward Beecher

> *After you have exhausted what there is in business, politics, conviviality, and so on – have found that none of these finally satisfy, or permanently wear – what remains? Nature remains.*
>
> Walt Whitman

Gradually, as I climbed higher, the view started to unfold. Most peaks were still draped with wisps of misty cloud. This slowly dissolved to reveal the savage scars of rock falls and shattered cliffs, remnants of a thousand storms. Exposed to snow, ice and wind, constantly deluged with rain, it looked as if the mountains had been sliced open and gutted, leaving suppurating wounds carved deep into their sheer bluffs. The upper peaks appeared awesome, aloof, ominous, and hinted of danger. More than a kilometer below me, I caught glimpses of the tiny silver ribbon that was my old friend the river, threading its way through the gorges and around the ends of the ridges.

I think that the leaf of a tree, the meanest insect on which we trample, are in themselves arguments more conclusive than any which can be adduced that some vast intellect animates Infinity.

Percy Bysshe Shelley

It wasn't difficult climbing and by mid afternoon I had traveled far enough to see, off in the distance, the small hut I was heading toward. Anticipating the warmth and shelter I'd soon experience there made me feel happy and complete. My wishes had been granted. I'd been provided with a clear day for this part of my journey. God is good! There was a spring in my step and many songs on my lips as I walked by a picturesque tarn (small lake) directly under one of the peaks I'd soon be climbing.

Silence is the element in which great things fashion themselves.

Maurice Maeterlinck

It was a particularly windswept spot. Even the moss had been blown away leaving only rocks. I reflected as I passed how horrible it would be here if it were windy and how glad I was I wouldn't be lingering when

Camp here.

I couldn't believe it. Did I hear right? Camp here?

Camp here.

I looked around, shocked. I'd never camped on the exposed tops before. This was early winter and a storm could blow up within an hour or two. Even in summer it is risky and foolhardy to stay on unsheltered peaks and ridges unless you can be certain of good weather. The last meteorological report I had heard some days before had predicted continual rain and cloud. My tent could probably withstand 80 kilometer per hour winds, but after that . . . ? I knew from the terrain that much worse could be expected. Although calm now, it could so quickly change and I'd be completely at the mercy of the fearsome gale force winds and perhaps be blown off the mountain. The safe thing to do would be to seek shelter in a lower gully, but that wasn't what was being asked of me.

Camp here.

I was terrified. On my own, exposed and vulnerable, my fears of what might happen

Give up the feeling of responsibility, let go your hold, resign the care of your destiny to higher powers, be genuinely indifferent as to what becomes of it all and you will find not only that you gain a perfect inward relief, but often also, in addition, the particular goods you sincerely thought you were renouncing.

William James

quickly escalated. I was being asked to put my life on the line! I never thought it would happen this way. Crossing a river, traversing a precipitous peak or bluff, yes – but not this, this cool, calculated suicide. I contemplated ignoring the call. Maybe I wasn't hearing right? Maybe it was all in my mind? But I knew this was a lie. Camping here broke every mountain craft rule I knew, went totally against common sense and exposed me to extreme danger. There was no way I'd think this one up myself. Besides, the call was so strong and clear I knew it was from a higher source.

What could I do? I was desperate, on the edge of panic, barely able to keep control. I didn't want this to be happening. I fell down on my knees and begged: "I'm so scared. I'm so afraid. Please God, anything but this, please, please!" I wept, groveled, implored and pleaded. I heard nothing – absolute silence.

After ten minutes or so of this pitiful display I was exhausted.

Then something changed. I don't know what happened, but a peace seemed to descend on me. Resigned to my fate I picked myself up and thought, "If I'm serious about abandoning my will power and learning to trust, I will have to go through with this. If

In your land it is regarded as a miracle if God does someone's will. In our country it is regarded as a miracle if someone does the will of God.

Anthony de Mello

You want me to die here, then so be it." Feeling like a condemned man I searched for an area with at least a modicum of shelter where I could pitch my tent.

Eventually I found a place among a few rocks that might give me some refuge from mild storms. Unfortunately, it was on very wet and soggy ground, a catchment area for the tarn. Still it was better than anywhere else. After erecting the tent and shifting all my gear inside, I began to feel a bit better. It began to snow lightly and within a few minutes the white snow collecting on the sides of my maroon tent made a pretty contrast. Somehow this comforted me.

It turned out to be only a passing squall so I wandered over to the other side of the ridge. There I sat and watched the cloud gently lift off the other peaks to reveal a cluster of mountains all dusted with snowy powdered sugar. Gradually the skies cleared completely and there on the skyline was the setting sun.

It was just on dusk and here before me was a staggeringly beautiful sunset framed between the now clear mountains. Being one of the southernmost countries in the world, New Zealand has exceptionally lengthy sunsets and twilights of two to three hours, depending on latitude. They seem to

The best remedy for those who are afraid, lonely or unhappy is to go outside, somewhere where they can be quiet, alone with the heavens, nature and God. Because only then does one feel that all is as it should be and that God wishes to see people happy, amidst the simple beauty of nature.

Anne Frank

go on forever. Captivated, I watched for hours until the last shreds of red and gold slipped from the sky. It was exquisite – a faultless symphony of radiant color. When the last remnants of pink finally dulled, I started crunching my way over the frost-covered rocks back to my tent when

Won't you stay with me just one more hour?

Christ's words to the disciples at Gesthemane. What could I do but stay? Entranced and somewhat incredulous of all that was happening, I turned around and walked further up the ridge. As I mounted the crest I was blasted (gob smacked would be a better description) by the full moon rising. Exorbitant! A total visual assault! I gasped at the extravagant beauty and wonder of it all and then took a grandstand seat to watch it slowly ascend.

As it was all those years before, here again was this uncanny combination of physical events and my emotional state producing a perfect union between nature, the divine, and me. I was overwhelmed by the sheer magnificence and sanctity of the moment. The moon seemed so much closer than usual, extraordinarily bright, as if especially lit up. It was just so precious, so personal, so perfect.

Beauty of whatever kind, in its supreme development, invariably excites the sensitive soul to tears.

Edgar Allan Poe

A miracle is an event which creates faith. That is the purpose and nature of miracles ... Frauds deceive. An event which creates faith does not deceive: therefore it is not a fraud, but a miracle.

George Bernard Shaw

I was flabbergasted at the sequence and timing of events that had to have taken place to bring me to this point to witness such a marvel: to be held in the valley for seven days and so be in this very spot on this day at this exact time; for the weather to clear and stay calm while I was there; for me to have been given enough faith that despite my terror I did what I was invited to do and camped; that I had been sufficiently trained to sit and wait in subzero temperatures in the dark rather than retreat to the warmth and comfort of my sleeping bag; that I had abandoned my will power and in return was given the courage to follow the calls.

At that moment I felt as if I were the luckiest man in the world. I was sitting on a volcano of splendor freely lavished on me, with no obligation to do anything at all except relish it. What else could I do? I had nothing to give that would ever repay this, I could never earn it. All that was required was for me to goggle at it and luxuriate in it. My appreciation was all my Own One seemed to want. But there was more to come.

I retired to bed, getting up four or five times during the night to relieve myself. Each time I noticed the moon as bright as ever tracking its course across the night sky. The last time I woke was not due to a full bladder, but to the sound of my mobile phone going off in my head!

Come and see.

By moonlight I walked to where I had seen the sun set the previous evening and this time observed the moon setting in the exact place! Again, amazing timing. After the last edge of the orb had slipped below the horizon I turned, and there rising where the moon had risen 12 or so hours ago, was the rising sun. Stunning! Incomprehensible! Thank you, thank you!

I witnessed the same phenomenon that evening and again the next morning. The weather continued to hold with only crisp, cool gentle mountain breezes accompanied by occasional wispy clouds. In this storm-racked region in early winter, I was being indulged with days on end of fine weather. It was unheard of and absurd. My dangerous campsite, the one I begged to be released from, the one where I was terrified I was going to die, had proved to be paradise.

To know that what is impenetrable to us really exists, manifesting itself as the highest wisdom and the most radiant beauty, which our dull faculties can comprehend only in their most primitive forms – this knowledge, this feeling, is at the centre of true religiousness. In this sense, and in this sense only, I belong to the rank of devoutly religious men.

Albert Einstein

NINE

The Source

I stayed three days on the crisp, cold mountain plateau. I was enjoying it so much that when lying in the mid-afternoon sun trying to soak up some warmth, and hearing the call to move on toward the hut, I resisted! "It's so nice here – can't I stay a bit longer?" But I knew that were I to stay, my fears of a few days ago, of being blown away by a storm, might become reality. Reluctantly, I packed up and moved on.

The breeze of divine grace is blowing upon us all. But one needs to set the sail to feel the breeze of grace.

Ramakrishna

As I climbed the weather began to deteriorate. Soon the cloud had completely closed in and I was barely able to see more than 100 meters. The wind increased too, buffeting me around as I followed the ridge line upward. At one point I walked over the same route I'd taken all those years before, past the point where I'd witnessed my friend lifted by the wind. However, this time it wasn't particularly difficult or dangerous climbing and I arrived within a few hours.

The hut had only been there 18 months and as such lacked character. I was struck by how empty and lonely it was. The starkness emphasized the loss of the intimate communion I'd been experiencing the last few days. I briefly wept for this and the unfamiliarity of such a manmade foreign place. With no one to be stoic for, my emotions were easy to express.

There's a disturbing element about mirrors, an icy unrelentingness. They lie in wait for us, catching us unawares, before we can pose. They're the great correctors – your indulgent idea of yourself is suddenly confronted with the truth.

Barry Oakley

There was a small mirror on the wall. I stood alongside it, so as not to catch my reflection, carefully removed the glass and placed it face down on the bench. It was ten days since I'd seen myself. Ten days since I'd had my image present itself and evaluate me with, "Too fat, too old, too tired." I much preferred my recent experiences of seeing myself through God's eyes. God's view is so much kinder, loving and more forgiving than mine.

The hut interior was spacious enough for me to stretch out my tent to dry. By the time I'd done this, arranged my bedding and cooked my daily packet of dehydrated food, I was feeling more at home. Once again the small things, the daily chores and rituals, gave a sense of belonging. Outside, the cloud and fog closed in, so I retired early.

I awoke to the sound of the mobile phone going off again. It was still dark.

Get up. Go up on the ridge.

I want to talk to you.

It wasn't easy. Icicles hung from the eaves and I was very warm and snug in my sleeping bag. A glance out the window showed it was quite cloudy, so a spectacular sunrise was out of the question. Why was I wanted on the ridge? Still, I was getting used to this and was excited about what I might find there. By the time I had dressed and put all my storm gear on, it was quite light. A few minutes later I was on the ridge top. I sat in the crisp, frost- stiffened snow grass braving the cold, to wait.

By now I was used to being held for hours, sometimes to see something, sometimes to hear, sometimes for no apparent reason. I wasn't sure what would be said, what I might learn, how long it would take before I was spoken to or if I'd be addressed at all. All I knew was I was open and ready and I had all day, all week if necessary, to wait. But no sooner had I sat down and begun to gaze into the steep valley that stretched out below me than,

You do not need to leave your room. Remain sitting at your table and listen. Do not even listen, simply wait. Do not even wait, be quite still and solitary. The world will freely offer itself to you to be unmasked, it has no choice, it will roll in ecstasy at your feet.

Franz Kafka

I am the source. Like the tarn in front of you that feeds this watershed. This spring, this stream, this river, lakes and oceans are all me. I am in them and they in me. In storms I replenish. All can dip into me as I flow past or lie still, yet I am also in them. Some hoard me, some love me, some dwell on my beauty, others use me. Some are locked in ice and snow for eons, others gush and bubble with me. Yet no matter how I am used I cherish all who take from me. Some will be plentiful with me and distribute me lavishly. Others will have to be squeezed to show any sign that I am there, yet none is greater or lesser, all are loved. This is my joy, my heart denied no one.

I offer it to all in full abundance. Take what you want and know forever that I am The Source.

Then alone do we know God truly, when we believe that God is far beyond all that we can possibly think of God.

St. Thomas Aquinas

I knew! I ran the image around in my mind, exploring the implications and the enormity of it. Of course! The sea, evaporation, osmosis in the plants, all living things have water in them. I tested the image and found more and more truth and wisdom in it. Profound, right, solid and true. Again and again I tested it against what I knew and each time it added to the knowing, until the words and my thoughts were interwoven, indistinguishable.

I was mesmerized by one of the most profound moments of my life. This was no revelation gleaned by my own thinking, the result of an intellectual logical process. It had been given as a "knowing." I knew, too, that this was no final definition. On the contrary, I'd had revealed but one drop in the ocean of this awesome and unfathomable concept. Combined with the knowing was an intense and unquenchable sense of support for me. It mattered not what I did, where I went or who I was, because I, too, was an integral part of this source. I sensed no separation between it, me, and anything else. An undiminished and complete part of it, as much as the mountains, plants, air and the water that inexorably flowed in the streams.

I was totally transported, cocooned. This was no passing moment, no fleeting spiritual or emotional high that would barely be remembered in years to come. What was happening now, this knowing, would never go. It was and always would be an extensive, entire and complete part of me.

It was nothing like the emotional surges of romantic love, the passion of lovemaking,

No statement about God is simply, literally true. God is far more than can be measured, described, defined in ordinary language, or pinned down to any particular happening.

David Jenkins

I would not say I believe. I know! I have had the experience of being gripped by something that is stronger than myself, something that people call God.

Carl Jung

or the ecstasy of chemically induced highs. This was totally different and beyond all my experience. It came from deep within, so deep that it stretched across time, THE time, solid and rooted to all that was and ever was to be. I felt humbled and privileged, yet worthy of at all at once. My emotional reference points no longer applied. It was as if the slate that was me had been wiped, yet I retained all my memories of it

I feel closer to what language can't reach.

Rainer Maria Rilke

As I write this, it is the same as when I was there. It is why I struggle with the word God. "God" just seems too small. It is lesser, definable, cloying, diminutive and excluding. What I experienced that day and from then on is expansive, inclusive, majestic and outrageous, an exorbitant and flagrant love, overwhelming in its capacity to accommodate and encompass anything – from the most monstrous evil to the highest good. All are contained by The Source. I didn't need to search for an understanding or definition of what I had experienced. I just knew.

TEN

Pinnacles

The revelation of The Source was still rever-
berating within me as I was invited to move
further down the ridge. Presently I came to
a wooden cross – a memorial erected over
30 years ago in memory of a hunter who had
died there during a storm, one of the many
tragic deaths in these mountains. I wondered what his last thoughts were on this
earth, as he lay lost, disorientated, lonely
and afraid, his life force ebbing away. As I
read the memorial plaque I allowed the
great sadness to overcome me. I wept for his
widow, for all the "could be's" that would
never be, for their unborn children and for
hopes gone cold.

With no others around there was no em-

I went to the woods because I wished to live deliberately, to front only the essential facts of life, and see if I could not learn what it had to teach, and not, when I came to die, discover that I had not lived . . .
I wanted to live deep and suck out all the marrow of life, to live so sturdily and Spartan-like as to put to rout all that was not life, to cut a broad swath and shave close, to drive life into a corner, and reduce it to its lowest terms.

Henry David Thoreau

barrassment, no one to be strong for, no one else's discomfort to consider. I was free to let the grief consume me and to openly show my sympathy by weeping. To express myself this way was liberating, if somewhat indulgent, but it seemed right. Death is so final, so profound a sorrow.

Head toward Arete.

I returned to the hut, packed my gear and headed off. An hour or so later I was traveling across a wide flat part of the ridge when again

Camp here.

I was annoyed by this. It was a clear, fine and cold day. I could see well, I had built up a brisk, rhythmic walking pace, and I felt I was really getting somewhere. This was my 11th day in the wilderness. More than a quarter of my time had elapsed and I still hadn't reached the mountain. In my mind, time was running out. I ignored the voice and kept on walking. For about 15 minutes I traveled but I was haunted. It was as if The Source was taunting me. It knew that as I grew accustomed to Its ways the invitations needn't be as strong. I could almost feel It sitting back and enjoying this.

You'll come round, you'll be back.

You know me too well to carry on.

I stopped, put down my pack and made

some conditions: "Only if I find a good camping spot."

I walked around and sure enough, within 100 meters I found a perfectly flat campsite.

"Only if there is fresh water." Again, within another 100 meters, I found a fresh spring. Obviously I was meant to stay here.

I put up my tent and spent the rest of the day sitting in the cool of the afternoon, wondering and contemplating. From where I sat I looked directly into a deep glaciated valley 500 meters below. I could faintly hear the tinkling of its stream, the only perceptible noise apart from the occasional buzz of a passing blowfly. I opened my coat and soaked up the sun, letting it caress and warm me. I felt mellow, cherished, and much loved. It was a glorious day, so crisp, clear and sunny I even took the opportunity to brave the cold and strip down for a wash.

As evening fell there was another beautiful sunset, but strangely the moon didn't rise straight away. (Somehow I'd gone through life without noticing that the moon rose at a different time each evening!) So later that night when I was wakened it made no sense at all.

Get up, pack up and go to Arete Bivvy.

I have learnt to love you late, Beauty at once so ancient and so new!

St. Augustine

I looked outside the tent and seeing the moon almost overhead I assumed it was about 2 a.m. By now I was used to the messages not revealing themselves immediately, but still I questioned it. Why should I get up and pack up in the freezing cold in the middle of the night? Still, who knew what this might lead to and I dearly wanted to trust and obey as the most feared part of my journey was coming up.

My chosen route traversed a set of pinnacles. For an hour or so I would encounter these precipitous and potentially dangerous peaks. On each side of the pinnacles was a 100 meter, almost vertical drop with no runout. If I slipped, there was nothing to prevent me from taking a major fall. I'd crossed here 20 years before, but back then I had a companion. It had been comforting to know that if one of us got into difficulties the other could assist. I also hadn't seen enough of life to realize the real danger I was in, or the actual risks we were taking. Now I well knew the hazards, but I faced them alone. I had been worrying about this for months. I'd repeatedly asked for fine weather when it was time to cross and the courage to face them on my own.

In my mind I'd built these pinnacles up to be a nearly impossible task. They were

If you wait for the perfect moment when all is safe and assured, it may never arrive. Mountains will not be climbed, races won, or lasting happiness achieved.

Maurice Chevalier

definitely dangerous and as I thought about them I recalled the words my son had said to me on our last phone call.

"There's no chance you'll fall off this here mountain is there, Pa?"

"No," I lied, "No chance."

I lied because I thought it the easy way out. I didn't want him to worry about me. I didn't want to be confronted by the puzzled, slightly incredulous look in his face that would imply, "You're going to deliberately expose yourself to danger and maybe even die? You're going to risk my father's life?" I lied because I couldn't face or defend myself against this quite accurate accusation.

Yet this "easy" way now plagued me. If I did fall, he would be totally betrayed. His father had lied to him. Why? A 15-word, ten-second conversation possessed me, nagged me, dogging my every move when near potential danger. "The truth will set you free." My so-called easy route had turned out to be the hard road. I was to discover this repeatedly over the next few weeks. Up here in solitude I had no one else to blame. My core habits were exposed; one of them being my quick fix attitude to avoid potential emotional pain. When viewed through my twin filters of laziness and pain avoidance, what looked easy often turned out to be

We fear that which we do not understand.

Anon

One of the most striking differences between a cat and a lie is that a cat has only nine lives.

Mark Twain

hard and vice versa. The fear of the pinnacles dwelled on my mind. There was no alternative route.

As I emerged from my tent into the moonlight I discovered that my boots, wet from the previous day's tramping through snow slush, had frozen solid. I loosened the laces and opened them as best I could, then stamped my feet down into them. They felt like wooden clogs. My tent, too, coated with frozen dew, had the texture of thick cardboard. I flicked off as much ice as I could and then, just as I was strapping it onto the outside of my rucksack, I noticed the sky lightening in the east. It was dawn – not the middle of the night as I had thought.

Religion is probably, after sex, the second oldest resource which human beings have available to them for blowing their minds.

Susan Sontag

Again this perfect timing because I'd listened and obeyed! If I'd trusted my own knowledge of the moon's habits I'd still be in bed. It began to dawn on me what Christ meant when he said, "I only do what I see the Father doing."

When I only did what I was called to do everything flowed so perfectly. Slightly incredulous, I started to think that maybe, just maybe, I too was tapped directly into The Source. Amazed, dazed and perplexed about how easy and clear it all seemed, I set off for the pinnacles.

In a few moments the first one loomed

right in front of me. In an hour or two I'd either be over them or lying in a bloody heap at the bottom. As I slowly climbed the first peak the dawn seemed to rise up with me. There wasn't a breath of wind nor any low cloud. I could hardly believe my "luck" to have the most wonderful day for the most feared part of my journey.

I slowly edged my way across the first two pinnacles. My heavy backpack exaggerated any slight loss of balance, so most of the time I made sure my hand- and footholds were doubly secure. On top of the third pinnacle I witnessed the sunrise. Perfect – the golden orb lighting up the valleys below. I felt welcomed by it, comforted by this sign that The Source was with me. I felt totally affirmed and approved of, and had a profound and deep sense of the rightness in being here. I stopped and gazed with passionate wonder. Golden rays penetrated the half-light, revealing the rippled ridges stretching out below me for as far as I could see.

Again and again I savored the extraordinary spectacle, almost spellbound by the beauty and my experience of it all. I say almost because I was still very, very afraid of the section I knew was going to be the toughest. This was where my dog had once

Caution has its place, no doubt, but we cannot refuse our support to a serious venture which challenges the whole of the personality. If we oppose it, we are trying to suppress what is best in man – his daring and his aspirations. And should we succeed, we should only have stood in the way of that invaluable experience which might have given a meaning to life. What would have happened if Paul had allowed himself to be talked out of his journey to Damascus?

Carl Jung

locked solid – plaintively whining, refusing to go forward or back. I'd had to carry him to where he felt more secure. Who would carry me today?

To my surprise I passed the feared trouble spot with no difficulty. The real problem lay on the last pinnacle. Snow, ice, wind and many footsteps had turned the route into a vertical shingle chute. There were few if any handholds, just crumbling rock. I glanced below. I had little chance if I fell. I tentatively started forward, inching my way ever so carefully over the crumbling rock. Suddenly, my outside foot slipped on the shingle. Momentarily I was caught off balance as my rucksack gathered momentum and swung me the wrong way, out and away from the cliff face. I was on my way down, slipping and sliding out of control.

Adversity introduces a man to himself.

Anon

Desperately I clawed at the gravel with both hands until I finally made contact with a rock that didn't move. For ages it seemed my whole life hung there relying on this one rock and the strength in my right arm. "Please God, please help, please!" The sinews in my shoulder were screaming as the combined weight of my body and pack hung on this single lifeline. I didn't dare lunge for fear of disturbing the rest of the gravel and loosening my lifesaving rock. My shoulder and arm pumped by adrenalin locked on and slowly, ever so gingerly, I pulled myself up, anticipating that at any second the rock would dislodge and I would begin tumbling down.

Eventually I gained a foothold, then another and another, until I arrived at the top, panting but safe. My heart pounding, the scenario of what had just happened re-played itself. No one was to pass that spot over the next four weeks. Injured or dead, I would not have been discovered until they came looking for me in 30 days time. It re-inforced what I already knew, that I couldn't totally rely on myself. I had no choice but to rely on other forces to save me.

So was I saved by God or by me? Who knows, but then is God possible without humanity or humanity possible without God? I know and I don't know. What I defi-nitely know is that of the hundreds of occa-sions I was afraid, this was only one of two incidents where what actually occurred jus-tified my fear. All the other times my fear was of what might happen.

But what an amazing, awesome sight I'd been saved for. On the summit I had a view worthy of kings. For this was one of the highest, clearest vantage points on the whole mountain range. I could see over 50

The misfortunes hardest to bear are those which never come.

J. R. Lowell

kilometers north, south and east with only the west obscured. One set of twin peaks about eight kilometers away had shafts of light boring out from behind them – what Renaissance painters called "the fingers of God." It looked radiant, like a gigantic stained glass window framing the altar of the twin peaks in the foreground. Here was an unsurpassed natural cathedral made perfectly, dare I believe made perfectly for me? Once again I was experiencing the incredible combination of nature, the divine, and me. I would have missed all this had I trusted my own knowledge of astronomy and stayed in bed. All this was mine simply because I responded to an invitation.

I am always most religious upon a sunshiny day...

Lord Byron

My whole being soared with wonder, with awe, with incredulity, for square kilometers of emptiness stretched out before me, with nothing human in sight. Dare I believe, dare I really believe that this was put here for me? It seemed a sacred moment – as if I was standing in a religious place. I was perched on top of a cathedral millions of years old, witnessing a celestial work in progress that would never be finished, yet was perfect in all its stages.

We must dare to think unthinkable thoughts.

J. William Fulbright

I began to sing any God song I could remember. Out they tumbled, the old hymns, gospel songs, church songs. I sang them softly and low so as not to break the sanctity of the silence that enveloped me. While I sang I pivoted round and round like a human radar dish, drinking in the different scenes as they unfolded about me. It was a primitive kind of church service; and it was Sunday, so what about the sermon? What else but the Sermon on the Mount? I recalled from memory what Jesus had said.

Consider the flowers and lilies. How beautiful they are. If something so small is cared for so well and bestowed with so much beauty, how much more will God care for you? You are blessed. Blessed beyond your wildest dreams. Though you may be poor, depressed, lonely, and heartbroken, I give you everything I have. Take it, enjoy it, it's yours. By loving my gifts you honor, please and love Me. In the same way you enjoy giving to your children I enjoy giving to you. Take it, drink it, eat it, be it – it's yours. I give unreservedly. There's nothing you can do or say that will stop me wanting to give you my all. Take it, love me, celebrate me, know me.

We have grasped the mystery of the atom and rejected the Sermon on the Mount.

 Omar N. Bradley

Again the messages of profoundly deep, total, selfless love. There were no hoops to jump through to receive it, no criteria to measure up to before I could take possession of it, no one else (especially myself) to judge whether I am worthy of it. There was no enlightenment needed – just take it. The beauty around me was unsurpassed, ecstatic, divine. I stood there for hours drinking it all in, having a ball – and I felt God, too, was having a ball. We celebrated and enjoyed each other. My soul magnified the Lord.

To love and be loved is to feel the sun from both sides.

David Viscott

ELEVEN

Being There

Eventually I moved on to the mountain that had been on my mind most of my life. Twelve days after I entered the ranges I finally arrived. Strangely, there was no sense of elation or satisfaction, in fact I felt an odd sense of dislocation. This was certainly no homecoming. It felt and looked like any other mountain. Perhaps it had been too long ago? Although I recognized and recalled the surroundings, the feelings weren't there. *C'est la vie.* I was becoming familiar with this unsettling sense each time I arrived somewhere new. I didn't like it but I knew it would pass.

The small bivouac hut that nestled below the summit had been moved a few

Solitude is un-American.
Erica Jong

meters since I was last there, but the view was the same. Opposite the door, 700 meters away over a steep ravine, was the V-shaped pass, just as I remembered it. Like most huts on the exposed tops, each corner of the roof was anchored to the ground by a tensioned wire. This was to hold everything in place when the full-force gales blew through. Battened down and huddled up in my storm refuge I was to be very thankful for this added security measure over the next few weeks.

We never seek things for themselves but for the search.

Blaise Pascal

The hut exterior was sound, but the interior was in poor condition. There was no fireplace as the nearest firewood was at least a couple of hours' walk below. Up here you kept yourself warm with whatever you had the foresight to bring with you. Green algae covered the walls and the floor was permanently wet as a tiny gap in one of the two windows allowed liters of water to come through every time it rained. With winds up to 200 kilometers per hour driving it, rain can pierce a pinhole.

The logbook showed few people staying, especially in winter. Often, months would go by between visits. That certainly boded well for my having uninterrupted solitude, but the lack of regular occupants meant that little maintenance had been carried out for a long time. This being the case I set about making my home for the next 28 days more habitable

I scraped the dirt and mud off the floor, buried the rubbish, and confined the rest of the hut junk to one corner. Using some black plastic I'd found, I managed to cover over the stain and filth on the small cooking bench. By the time I had laid out my sleeping mat and bag on one of the two bunks it felt a lot more welcoming. As with fetching wood and picking up rice, the cleaning made me care more.

Trust in God and keep your powder dry.
Oliver Cromwell

The friendly puttering of my Primus also comforted me. This cooking stove was 26 years old, the only piece of equipment I still retained from my original trip. It had been with me through many wet, cold and tough adventures, constantly providing hot meals, hot drinks and comfort. This never failing friend had consoled me then, and now triggered familiar feelings of warmth and sustenance.

I was on the eastern "sheltered" side of the mountain, about a 20-minute, easy climb to the summit. From where I now stood, in front of the hut, there was a magnificent panorama of mountains. I stayed there all afternoon gazing across to where I'd been five days before, where I'd been asked to "camp here." I could see from this vantage point that the camping spot was on one of the best viewing platforms in the whole dress circle of mountains. I had been placed in the finest box seat, there to be dazzled by an astonishing visual symphony. I marveled again at the privilege, the indescribable experience and immaculate timing that took place, and the profound sense, for once in my life, of having gotten something absolutely, perfectly right!

As I sat and the shadows started to fall, I began to make plans to go up to the summit. This would be my first opportunity to get an unobscured view of the whole mountain range and out to the sea. Since it had been such a clear, still afternoon I expected to catch a great sunset, a magnificent curtain call to a fantastic day when

Don't go up there tonight.

What?

Don't go up there tonight. There is great danger for you. Stay here.

I couldn't believe it! Calm, clear conditions, no ice, only a sprinkling of snow – how on earth could it be dangerous? I ran the voice information through all the checks to make sure I was hearing from the right Source.[1] Was it consistent? Clear? Loving? Or something I'd logically worked out? Yes, yes,

Reason is our soul's left hand, Faith her right, By these we reach divinity.

John Donne

yes, no. It definitely wasn't what I wanted to hear. I'd spent nearly two weeks getting here, had planned and waited months, the weather was perfect, and I knew it was highly unlikely to stay clear, so I checked it out again.

Why not go up there? It looks great to me.

Tonight's dangerous. Stay here.

Why? What's so dangerous about it?

Bad juju, danger for you tonight.

How can there be? It's a marvelous evening!

The conversation went on like this, to and fro, for the next 20 minutes or so.

I was not at all pleased about missing out on what promised to be an exquisite evening and I wasn't about to give in quickly. I was champing at the bit. What could be better than celebrating together this wonderful world with my, and its, Maker? Surely The Source wanted me to enjoy it? So I hit on a "compromise." I promised to be very careful. It seems laughable now, but at the time it seemed logical to me. I was on such a high from the morning that I thought I was invincible. I hated the thought of missing out. But then

If you go up there tonight you'll fall

Faith certainly tells us what the senses do not, but not the contrary of what they see; it is above, not against them.

Blaise Pascal

---

[1] See Appendix 1.

to your death.

That clinched it for me. It couldn't get much clearer than that! I was still curious, however, about how I could fall on such a calm day. The walk to the summit is really quite easy with only a few places that are slightly precipitous. There are plenty of footholds, and substantial runout areas should I slip. I was puzzled, but I heeded the warning.

The next day as I strolled to the summit I was shown the spot where I would have fallen.

*Here. Here's where you would have
fallen to your death*

It looked innocuous enough to me. It was a moderate slope with plenty of room to easily arrest a fall. Strange, yet the voice had been so consistent and clear. It was not unitl a few weeks later that I discovered what might have been.

It was another clear, cold evening. (Yes, there were many more days of fine weather.) I was sitting on the summit watching the sun set over the sea. Enraptured, I waited until it had completely gone, leaving me seated there in total darkness. Rising to return to the hut, I reached into my parka pocket to retrieve my flashlight and to my horror discovered the zip was jammed. Here I was, totally alone, miles from the nearest other human, even further from civilization, in the dark freezing cold, without a flashlight and with no way of getting back to safety. I felt the panic begin to rise up in me. My Gore-Tex ® parka had rip-proof fabric so it would take me ages to tear it, if I could manage it at all. Because it was dark I couldn't see what was jamming the zip. I felt doomed. Would I survive a night out on the mountain? I didn't want to have to find out. Within a few moments I'd been catapulted from awe, contentment and wonder, into the icy corridors of panic and unrestrained terror. Suddenly I felt very, very afraid and very, very alone.

Eventually some inner strength took charge of me and gently lowered my panic. An elder, more experienced Guide took me sensitively through the steps

Take your gloves off. Gently work on the zip. If necessary cut your coat with your knife.
It'll be okay. We're with you.

My voice or God's? I don't know, but it was right. I could now feel that the cloth pull-tabs of both the coat and pocket zips were jammed together.

Through gentle rather than panic

To me the sole hope of human salvation lies in teaching Man to regard himself as an experiment in the realization of God, to regard his hands as God's hand, his brain as God's brain, his purpose as God's purpose. He must regard God as a helpless Longing, which longed him into existence by its desperate need for an executive organ.

George Bernard Shaw

stricken maneuverings, I managed to open the pocket just enough to squeeze out the small but powerful flashlight. Considerably sobered, I began walking back down toward the hut. I shone the light over the spot where I was told I would have fallen that first night. I could see no danger when I was fit and well, with fully functioning equipment. But now, in the dark and cold with the wind rising as quickly as my panic, I realized how and why I may have met my demise. I sensed little risk when the sun shone brightly and the wind was low, but they could, those who watched over me.

TWELVE

Who's There?

So who was this "They" who watched over me? All along I'd assumed the inner voice to be God, or my concept of a personal God, which it may well have been. But since the revelation of The Source, there now seemed to be so much more going on in the spiritual realm, a virtual supernova explosion of love. In the ensuing weeks on the mountain my way of addressing the Holy One didn't change, but I became more aware that the way I was spoken to varied from an anonymous voice, to singular, to plural. There was no pattern, no formula, just consistent themes:

We love you...We are watching over you...I want to get closer to you...

Make friends with the angels, who though invisible are always with you... Often invoke them, constantly praise them, and make good use of their help and assistance in all your temporal and spiritual affairs.

St. Francis de Sales

*Thank you for coming...We are with
you... I will soothe your hurt...We
are caring for you...It is enough that
you are here...You're doing all
right...We're proud of you*
There were also gentle invitations
Listen to the wind...
Just watch the light...
Look at the rock...

As I pondered these invitations and thoughts unceasingly, something would gradually become clear. There was no doubting that God was in all this, but it was a much bigger celestial communication channel than I had ever suspected – insepa- rable, but somehow also apart. Strange, mysterious.

One morning toward the end of my stay I was wakened by this:

*In the early morning before it got
light he took himself off to a quiet
place to pray.*

The remnants of the night's storm were still growling so I chose to go to a rock grotto about ten minutes walk away from the hut. It would be sheltered enough for me to stay as long as might be required. Donning all my storm gear and walking through the driving rain I soon arrived at the rock hol- low. There I shuffled around a bit to find

Just as in earthly life lovers long for the moment when they are able to breathe forth their love for each other, to let their souls blend in a soft whisper, so the mystic longs for the moment when in prayer he can, as it were, creep into God.

Søren Kierkegaard

somewhere reasonably comfortable to sit, and within minutes

> *Go and prepare yourself for the Lord. Wash your hands and face and teeth in the stream, then return to the cabin and wait for Him there.*

I did as I was asked, washed in the stream and then returned and tidied the hut. I swept it out and then laid my small purple towel on the bench as a kind of rough altar cloth. Lighting the purple candle I had put aside for special sacred times, I knelt and prayed, "Lord, we welcome you here, the Holy Spirit, all the angels and all the forces of good." The rough hut seemed to take on a special sanctity, I felt humbled, expectant, and in awe.

Quietly, softly, reverently I sang *So come,* closed my eyes and…there was the presence of the Christ seated in front of me holding His hand out. I put my head on his chest and cried. All the fear, worry and pain melted into Him as He stroked my head.

Thou hast touched me and I have been transformed into thy peace.

St. Augustine

> *We all love you. Well done, good and faithful servant.*

Later I was asked to kneel.

> *This is my yoke on your shoulders. See how perfectly it fits. That's because it was made especially for you…*

Please stay with me

I am with you always, to the ends of the earth.

And then He was gone, but He wasn't. The Presence was still with me even though It had departed. I felt touched, special, humbled and deeply, deeply loved. I was in heaven.

So was it angels that had asked me to prepare? Was it the "Holy Spirit" that had guided me? I don't know, but what I do know is that the voices were just as valid and clear as the *other* voice. A voice that cajoled, threatened, accused, inspired fear, sowed seeds of doubt, made me work harder, exhorted me to do it on my own, to rely on my individual strength and resources – in short, a voice that did anything and everything to separate me from The Source, often with a lot of help from myself.

It was an evening, some days earlier. The storm had been raging for three days. Cooped up in my hut I had a case of cabin fever, so I was eager to hear a call, any call.

Go to the tarn, there's something I want you to see.

Why? What's there?

Just go and look.

The words and expression were similar but something just didn't feel right. Still I'd been wrong before and I really wanted to believe it was The Source, as I was bored and restless. I wondered what might be up there. Maybe a deer? That was it. A deer was going to come down and drink at the tarn and I was being invited to see it.

The tarn was a small lake about 15 minutes walk from the hut. Measuring approximately 30 meters by ten meters, it was quite picturesque. On fine days it reflected the mountains, but since it had become iced over, it had taken on an irregular "crazy" paving appearance. But to get to it now, in storm conditions, meant putting on all my protective gear. The rain and sleet were still being blown horizontally, incessantly hammering the hut and anything else foolish enough to be exposed to the weather.

As I pulled on extra layers of clothing, overtrousers and snow gaiters, I started to get excited. Building in my mind the wonderful sight of watching a deer come down to drink at the tarn right at dusk, I played with the idea that I was some sort of St. Francis of Assisi, a friend to all animals. I believed in my own blessedness to produce a miracle on command as I hungered for something, anything, to happen.

Fully convinced, off I went. To say it was unpleasant would be an understatement. The sleet stung my face. I constantly slipped and

It is easy – terribly easy – to shake a man's faith in himself. To take advantage of that to break a man's spirit is devil's work.

George Bernard Shaw

Each one of us – every soul – is a battle-ground for a struggle between good and evil.

M. Scott Peck

missed my footing, falling many times. The wind chill factor worsened the already bitterly cold conditions. Struggling against the wind, using all my own tough-it-out strength, I finally arrived and sat down beside the tarn to await the deer I was now fully convinced would materialize before my eyes.

As the buffeting wind tugged at my clothes, its howling cold sapping what little warmth I had, I waited and waited. Soon I became frustrated and angry. "What's going on here? You called me out here to see one of your creatures and nothing's happening. I'm really confused…"

Instantly I realized my mistake. Clarity not confusion is The Source's style. I had been cleverly deceived because I was so eager to believe. I hadn't paused and checked who the message was from. I had picked up and run with the idea because it appealed to me. It was something I really wanted to happen, so much so that I hadn't even tried to verify it because I might have received an answer I didn't want to hear. I hadn't scrutinized the information because I was hell-bent on relieving the monotony.

He got me didn't he?

Yup.

Suckered wasn't I?

Sure were.

How often in my life have I leapt on my own or the accuser's ideas and run away with them? How often have I compromised, twisted and distorted The Source's wishes to suit myself? How often The Master must sigh and wonder why, despite all evidence to the contrary, I continue to place faith in my own shortsighted, narrow judgements. How often have I missed out on inexhaustible good fortune because I did it my way? How often have I been forgiven? How often have I had my mistakes accommodated and smoothed over?

But now I laughed at my own naivety, and at how easily I'd been duped. As I gratefully walked back to warmth and shelter, I felt the Great Presence surround and comfort me. Both of us were enjoying my mistake and celebrating the lesson learned. There was not a word of condemnation, no recrimination that I had been well and truly suckered, just joy in having me back to bask in love.

So who's talking here? Who are "They"? I can only guess. I am reluctant to ascribe any label, as the Loving Presence is so vast, so all-consuming, so powerful, so explosively compassionate that words seem stupidly inadequate or pathetically clumsy. Perhaps the confusion is intentional so we

God is more truly imagined than expressed and He exists more truly than is imagined.

St. Augustine

The supreme happiness of life is the conviction that we are loved – loved for ourselves, or rather, loved in spite of ourselves.

Victor Hugo

don't fall into the trap of putting The Source into a human pigeonhole, thereby making it something we can define, claim or own. Maybe we're not supposed to know. Maybe bits will be revealed as we are ready for them. I really don't know. But I do know how much I am loved.

THIRTEEN

Food and Art

Day 13 arrived, the first on my special mountain. Weatherwise it wasn't great. Wisps of scattered cloud and mist drifted in and out obscuring the views, particularly of the pass. For some reason I felt very dispirited. I'd begun to notice that being on my own and withdrawn from the world tipped me toward more childlike patterns of behavior. Free to express, rather than repress, my emotions, I fluctuated between exuberance and despair, contentment and frustration, passion and complacency. In the civilized adult world I usually inhabit, this emotional see-sawing would be unacceptable. When surrounded by others, I apply the tried and true passion and de-

If you carry your childhood with you, you never become older.

Abraham Sutzkever

spair neutralizers: denial, sophistication and bland stoicsm.

I was quite downhearted. The lack of food wasn't helping. On fine days or when I was traveling, I hardly ever thought about food and ate very little. Mesmerized as I was by the magnificent scenery unfolding in front of me, I had only occasional thoughts of eating. In normal life my appetite is constantly stimulated by an endless array of goodies from cafés, supermarkets, bread shops and my fridge. I find it very hard to resist the temptation to graze on all these tasty morsels when everywhere I look something is saying "eat me, eat me." The fact that I didn't desire food on the mountain showed me how much my eating is just a reaction to stimulus, a habit, a routine. Out of sight was truly out of mind.

However, my empty stomach did have a dulling effect on me. I only became aware of this when I noticed a marked contrast in my mood as soon as I had eaten – generally a warm feeling of contentment coupled with a more positive outlook. Despite this, I never had hunger pains and hardly ever craved food. It was the same for sex. Without the stimulus, it just wasn't an issue.

I had it in my mind that once I reached the mountain it might be a good idea to fast.

Staying put as I was, with no huge calls on my energy, it seemed safe enough to do so. If I started eating a few days before I began my long journey out, I reasoned I should build up sufficient strength to cope with the energy demands. The previous day, Day 12, I hadn't eaten anything, so in a way I'd already begun fasting. I put it up for examination.

Shall I fast?

Why?

So I can trip[1] with You, lose weight, and be more attractive to Christine.

You'll be attractive to Christine whether you fast or not, and anything I'm going to reveal to you will be done with or without a full stomach.

Thank God for that! As I was going to discover, storm days without food were hell. Eating provided one of the few reliefs to the monotony of being confined indoors for days on end and completely hut bound. I found the trick was to delay breakfast as long as possible, so that the gap between eating my two daily meals became quite bearable. However, today food didn't seem to be the problem, I just felt miserable.

On the skyline about 70 meters or so above the hut was a grotesquely shaped

The belly is the reason why man does not mistake himself for a god.

Friedrich Nietzsche

---

[1]After about three days of fasting, hallucinations are quite common.

rocky outcrop. Silhouetted, it looked like a gargoyle, so when I was told to take a wander and wonder I meandered my way up there. I discovered a huge natural granite sculpture, about four meters high and three meters thick. Carved by ice, it was a legacy of the glaciers that would have been here during the last ice age. There were quite a few of these sculptured rocks in the area, but this particular one was by far the biggest. I stopped and stared at it for quite a while, as I would with any other work of art. Eventually I tired of this and turned to walk away when

Look at the sculpture.

I paused and considered it more thoroughly, walking around it, looking at it from this angle then that, but try as I might I couldn't see anything significant.

There's something I want you to see.

I was eager to see what was so special about it for I had experienced a similar revelation a week earlier.

Down beside the river, the day before I started my ascent, I had been invited to stay a while with my Own One. I watched the water lapping the shoreline for quite a while and then I noticed one rock was shaped in a very similar way to Michaelangelo's depiction of Moses. As the

Your vision will become clear only when you look into your heart. Who looks outside dreams. Who looks inside awakens.

Carl Jung

flood level receded and the water level dropped, I continued to study the rock, which eventually revealed "Moses" holding what looked like a dead lamb. I gazed into the expression on the old man's face. What resolute determination it showed, aggrieved but not bitter, a kind of sadness.

As I continued to examine the image and play with the ideas it evoked, I became aware I was seeing a depiction of God's face holding up the "broken lamb," The Christ. Like Michaelangelo's *Pieta*, it captured for me some of the profound loss, mourning and sacrifice involved in the passion, underpinned by superhuman love. It was quite moving and very, very powerful, as it reflected some of the enormous pain involved

It was quite a coincidence to see it, for it required the water levels and afternoon light to fall in a particular way before the image became apparent. The next morning just before climbing, I had returned to say farewell to the river sculpture, but with different light and water levels, it carried little of its previous presence.

Suspecting that the image in the granite I was now being asked to look for might be as transitory as the river sculpture, I began to get a bit impatient. "Give me a clue here – what do you want me to see?"

Sorrow makes us all children again, destroys all differences of intellect. The wisest knows nothing.

Ralph Waldo Emerson

Dios tarda pero
no olvida.
*God delays
but doesn't forget.*

Spanish Proverb

It's about the crucifixion.

From where I now stood I couldn't see anything like the crucifixion. I looked all over, screwed up my eyes, held my fingers up to block off various bits, but nothing appeared. Eventually I got bored, gave up and moved on. It was getting too hard. I figured if it was really so important it would eventually be revealed when I had been given the eyes to see.

Three days later I passed by the sculpture again and there was the crucifixion! Mary was weeping at the foot of the cross, one of the disciples was lowering Christ's body – profound, sombre, and very moving. Around the back, high up behind Christ's head, was a slightly protruding rock about the size of a small pumpkin; in it I could see the perfect face of an infant. As I stared at the child's daintily carved features, I noticed that it changed. As in an optical illusion, the child's face turned into a young woman's, and then back again. I couldn't see both at the same time. I scrutinized the image and tossed around the ideas it stirred up. Both the child and the young woman had terribly sad faces. Could one be the unborn, unkept infant? Perhaps the stillborn or the infant that died in childbirth?

*Sorrow's the great
community in which
all men born of
woman are members
at one time
or another.*

Sean O'Casey

Could it be the young woman had to give

her child away? Whatever it was, there seemed to be a profound sorrow surrounding the whole statue, both crucifixion and infant. I called it the Statue of Sorrows.

I revisited this Statue of Sorrows many times in the ensuing weeks as it was on my route to the summit. On each occasion I would pause and let the anguish touch me. Late one afternoon I looked harder at the clusters of rocks nearby and discovered they too offered depictions of grief and woe; the wife draped over her husband's tomb, the lonely and destitute huddled figure of the rejected refugee, the dumb blank empty look on one man – a lifetime of total grief and despair. Then there was another one I discovered one evening a few days before I left; the head of a man and a woman as clear and as lifelike as Rodin would sculpt. The husband was howling his anguish to the heavens, as he clasped his wife's dead, lifeless head between his hands.

Can I see another's woe, And not be in sorrow too?
William Blake

Death, pain, loss, and profound misery. All around me were sorrows, a virtual garden of sorrows. I moved among them touching each one, murmuring "I'm sorry" and in turn letting their sadness touch me. I wept alongside them and for them, for what other response was there? So many sorrows, so many sadnesses. Is this what The Creator sees? How

Not a day passes over the earth but men and women of no note do great deeds speak great words and suffer noble sorrows.
Anon

does The Source contain and console these incredible sufferings? I had been given a glimpse into the miseries of the world. It was a painful and necessary privilege, for suffering is an integral part of life.

FOURTEEN

Blessings in Disguise

One hundred meters beyond and above the garden of sorrows was the crest of one of the ridges that eventually lead on to the summit. Arriving there later in the morning on Day 13, I sat down to watch and contemplate. I felt empty and despondent, quite downhearted and I didn't know why.

I hoped I would soon experience some of the delight of solitude I'd previously enjoyed. Gazing through the mist into the shingle scree slide below, I was momentarily distracted when I thought I caught some movement. What could it be? A deer perhaps? I'd seen plenty of droppings and footprints. The cloud parted briefly to reveal it was no deer, but someone walking slowly

If what you seek is Truth, there is one thing you must have above all else . . . an unremitting readiness to admit you may be wrong.

Anthony de Mello

Be not forgetful to entertain strangers: for thereby some have entertained angels unawares.

New Testament

in my direction! I couldn't believe it! I had come all this way to one of the most isolated places in the mountains, it was midweek and here was someone else!

I panicked. I didn't want this to be happening. I had been through so much to get to this stage. It had been seven days since my brief encounter with the others down at the river, which had been caused, I thought, by ignoring an invitation. This time I couldn't think of anything I had, or hadn't done that might have put me out of kilter with The Source. I thought I'd been totally obedient and in tune. Seeing this stranger put me into a state of shock. I quietly asked what I should do. Nothing came to me. Silence.

If you hear nothing do nothing.

I stayed still for a few minutes until it became too much for me. I just had to do something. It was so unexpected it had thrown me completely. I was confused and panicked.

Run quick, run away.

Like a frightened fawn I took off around the other side of the ridge hoping whoever it was hadn't seen me. After 100 meters or so I slowed my mad dash and walked cautiously back to the hut via a circuitous route around the other side of the mountain. As I walked I hoped, wished and prayed I had been mistaken, that I'd just been seeing things, or that whoever it was was just passing by. Why was I cursed by this interruption? Wasn't I supposed to be in solitude? I still had a lot to learn.

Finally a message penetrated through my tortured jumble of thoughts.

This is the stranger, welcome him.

I did so and what a delight he turned out to be! Edwin, a Dutchman in his early 30s, had spent the previous night under a rock shivering in the rain. He'd missed the hut he was aiming for and was pleased to finally find some shelter. He was quite an adventurer. He'd spent two years cycling from Alaska to Chile and was planning a return visit to South America to walk 2000 kilometers along one of the old Inca trails.

Throughout the day we chatted, covering all the great topics like work, women, and the meaning of life. As we talked, I began to realize his arrival here was no coincidence. He made computer circuit boards and I made films. Both were creative pursuits and I completely agreed with his insight that true creativity lies in deciding what to throw away rather than what to include. He also reckoned truth was beauty and beauty truth. He'd read all the great

Always judge a person by the way he treats somebody who can be of no use to him

Anon

*Every time a man
unburdens his heart
to a stranger he
reaffirms the love that
unites humanity.*

Germaine Greer

*I have always
depended on the
kindness of strangers.*

Tennessee Williams

philosophers but still hadn't found THE truth. I asked him how he'd know it when he came across it, but he let that one pass.

I shared with him my reasons for being there, and some of the things I'd experienced. I told him that I'd done everything I'd ever wanted to do and I wasn't sure what to do next. That I had lost touch with who I was, why I was on earth, and where I was heading. I had lost my way and with it much of my passion for life. He was quite surprised: "But you have an incredible passion to tell, it just flows out of you!"

Bingo! It was as if someone had turned on the floodlights. The mist of my confusion instantly evaporated. Here, completely out of the blue, was an affirmation of my passion, of who I really was. Edwin was right! I loved telling. From the time I was a small boy when my patient mother listened to my tall tales, to my work as a film maker, I reveled in telling. I love stories. I love processing and reworking information, reassembling it so it's more readily understood. It's who I am. I'd simply die if I couldn't tell it!

Buoyed up by this discovery and fueled by the first caffeine hit I'd had for two weeks, I rocketed up to the summit to catch the sunset. Already on a massive high from Edwin's insight, I crested the summit to catch my first unobscured view of the entire mountain range. I gasped. I could hardly believe it. For there was much more than just the ranges I stood on; 150 kilometers to the north I could clearly see the impressive snowcapped volcanoes, bathed in magenta and crimson. Another 150 to the south lay another range of imposing snowcapped alps. Directly in front of me was the sun: golden, then crimson, then purple as it sank into the Tasman Sea.

On a fine, clear day like the one I was enjoying, New Zealand sunsets are utterly breathtaking. I gazed in awe. What can rival the sun setting into the sea viewed from the top of a mountain on a clear day? It was absolutely majestic, imposing, and wonderful. Thank you, thank you! As I sat there celebrating the Maker's works, and thankful for the dazzling display, I felt as if I was being thanked for enjoying it! The Source was gaining immense pleasure from my pleasure. I hummed and sang any love song that came to mind, trying to express the inexpressible gratitude, amazement, and awe I was feeling. The Platters *Only You*, Elvis Presley's *Can't Help Falling in Love*, Jimmy Barnes' (*Your Love Keeps Lifting Me) Higher and Higher*, Joe Cocker's *You Are So Beautiful*. Songs seemed the only way to touch what I felt.

And so he who would lead a Christ-like life is he who is perfectly and absolutely himself. He may be a great poet, or a great man of science, or a young student at a university, or one who watches sheep upon a moor, or a maker of dramas, like Shakespeare, or a thinker about God, like Spinoza; or a child who plays in a garden, or a fisherman who throws his net into the sea.

Oscar Wilde

If the only prayer you say in your whole life is "thank you," that will suffice.

Meister Eckhart

*The soul can split the
sky in two,
And let the face of God
shine through.*

Edna St. Vincent
Millay

As I sang each song over and over they seemed to transform somehow until I realized that what I was singing to The One had been turned around and was now being sung back to me! Was there no end to this riot of love for me? I was incredulous at how it all worked in so perfectly.

As the first star appeared I made my usual first-star wish: "I wish that God and me are like this" (fingers crossed over each other). How my wishes had come true, how my prayers had been answered, in spite of my best efforts to thwart them by running away! I had been sent a human messenger to console and affirm me, a physical presence to speak real words of affirmation and love The Source knew I needed to hear. Luckily, this time there hadn't been anywhere to run to. Unfortunately, the next time there was.

FIFTEEN

A Hard Lesson

Edwin left the next day, but a few days later another group came by. The party of three, including a teenage girl, didn't have suitable windproof mountain clothing and they arrived practically done in. Staying too long on the exposed tops, their hands had become so cold their fingers wouldn't function. But instead of welcoming the strangers and offering them a warm brew to cheer them up, I vacated the hut as quickly as possible. I ran away so as to maintain my solitude. My behavior was quite shameful, I thought only of myself.

Initially I was going to camp near the hut, but as I prepared to do so

Why not go and camp down in Arete

Most of man's trouble comes from his inability to be still.

Blaise Pascal

stream?

I liked that idea. I reasoned it would be a lot warmer down in the valley among the trees and it would be nice to hear a friendly river again. Besides, seeing as I was already on the move why not move further, to somewhere more hospitable? Who knows, it may even lead to an adventure.

I didn't stop to consider where this thought had come from or to check if it was what I was supposed to do. Somehow the arrival of the strangers had thrown me into "go" mode, so I flung my gear into my backpack and took off.

Experience is a hard teacher. She gives the test first and the lessons afterward.

English proverb

It was late afternoon when I left. If I kept up a good pace, the marked route down to the stream should take me about two and a-half hours. I thought that looked too hard and too long, so I took what I thought would be an easier, shorter way. There was no track on this "short cut," but that didn't deter me; I was on a mission. At first all went well and I was feeling quite pleased with myself. "The old body can still crack it on when it has to," I smugly thought. And then I hit the tree line. My progress was abruptly stopped by a dense band of leatherwood, a short tough scrubby bush that is exactly the wrong height – too tall to go over, too short to walk under, and too tough to push through.

The only way to progress is to crawl through its branches, a tedious frustrating and time-consuming exercise, one that is made much harder as your backpack continually gets hung up on the branch just above you. The more you push, strain and shove, the more energy it stores up in these branches to spring you back to where you were a few minutes before. To make it even more laborious, the leatherwood is usually growing on a very steep slope.

For hours it seemed I battled through this impenetrable barrier, gaining only a few hundred meters in the process. I'd also suffered a few falls and it began to dawn on me that going off the beaten track like this and getting hidden in an impenetrable thicket in one of the remote parts of the ranges was not a very sensible thing to be doing. Should I fall and sustain injuries that would prevent me from moving, I'd never be found. I remembered how much I had insisted I wanted to be alone. No one would come looking for me for weeks, by which time… Funny how I hadn't thought of this before! I hadn't even given it a second thought before I plunged off the track. By now it was almost dark and I still had to find a campsite. Things were not good.

Where was The Source in all this? I'd

There are times when we must sink to the bottom of our misery to understand truth, just as we must descend to the bottom of a well to see the stars in broad daylight.

Václav Havel

Much knowledge of things divine escapes us through want of faith.

Heraclitus

Guilt has very quick ears to an accusation.

Henry Fielding

simply tuned out. When I'd realized I hadn't listened, trusted or complied, I felt sheepish about my mistake and I had quickly switched channels, filling my head with enough static to prevent any meaningful spiritual communication. It was a very common behavior of mine and one I'd been challenged about before. After the first few days and nights on the tops I had felt jaded by the enormity of all the "big calls." Scared there'd soon be another big ask, I'd switched off. Eventually, my self-generated static cleared enough for me to hear

We'd rather you said "no" than tuned us out.

They missed me! This time I kept the spiritual realms at arm's length for as long as I could, but it was no use. I seemed to be hounded by recriminations, scorned and taunted about how I had got it wrong. Embarrassed by my behavior toward the strangers, bitterly disappointed in myself for not listening, exasperated by my lack of progress, and exhausted by the physical struggle I broke down and wept.

"All right!" I shouted. "I made a mistake. I'm sorry all right! Just leave me alone will you, leave me alone!"

Tears of frustration, self-loathing, disappointment and shame flowed. I had abandoned my guide and confidant, betrayed my best friend and I didn't know why.

I was experiencing a horrible sense of being totally alone. Just me, solo against the elements. My crash-through, tough-it-out philosophy was fine when things were going well, but once things came unstuck I was left with a disturbing emptiness – a void in my soul. And now it looked as if darkness would overtake me before I could locate a suitable tent site. The cold wind laughed at my frailty.

It's not me who's mocking you.
Don't give up. We're with you.
Come on, it'll be all right. You're nearly there.

Words of love, words of tenderness. There were no reprimands, no rebukes, no chastisement, just support and love. Humbled, tired, and slightly cheered, I carried on and just at dusk I found a campsite. This hadn't been one of my better days.

The next morning I was woken up by
Pack up and go back to Arete Bivvy.

After my behavior yesterday, it seemed as if The Source was taking much firmer control. According to the map, the best route back to the bivouac was to head downriver for a couple of kilometers until it intersected a track that led back up the

Ah, mon cher, for anyone who is alone, without God and without a master, the weight of days is dreadful.

Albert Camus

To will what God wills is the only science that gives us rest.

Henry Wadsworth
Longfellow

We have been looking for the burning bush, the parting of the sea, the bellowing voice from heaven. Instead we should be looking at the ordinary day-to-day events in our lives for evidence of the miraculous.

M. Scott Peck

mountain. This time I was going to take the long way. I was taking no chances today and neither was my Guide. Keeping in close contact, I'd constantly check my movements, admire the scenery, stop when called on to delight in the beautiful deep, clear green pools. It felt so good to be back in step with the true Master, walking along keeping in tune with the perfect rhythms of grace.

Presently the river ran into a gorge dropping vertically to become a spectacular waterfall, but alas, one too dangerous to climb down. There was no alternative but to climb up and out of the gorge and hopefully intersect the track. It wasn't easy. The water splashed, moss-covered walls had few secure hand- and footholds, but I pushed my way up and then began the vertical climb up the canyon walls. Soon there were enough trees to cling to, but it was tough going. Yesterday's episode of floundering through the leatherwood had drained me of much of my energy reserves. This was Day 19 on reduced rations and it showed up in a markedly diminished zeal. I asked for The Source's strength and power to carry me on as mine was quite limited.

Rest

I gratefully sank down and was pleasantly surprised by a couple of fat native pi-

geons and three Tuis or parson birds (so
named for the tuft of white feathers under
their necks). I'd not seen these two species
so close together before. They put on quite
a display, especially the Tuis singing their
lungs out. It was as if the critters were cheering me on, reminding me I was not alone,
that my Own One was with me saying "Welcome back." I certainly had none of the
sense of loneliness I'd experienced the day
before. Maybe The Source was a good ter-
restrial guide as well as a celestial one? I
abandoned map and compass and asked
that I be guided.

Go left, keep left, go left.

I gave it a go. If I were navigating I would
have gone straight up, not left, but remark-
ably I soon hit the track. I had been saved
another exhausting, leatherwood bush-
bashing episode.

Rest.

I stopped and sat down. Immediately a
small bird joined me. It was enchanting –
chirping and warbling, it almost sat on me
in its excitement. It made me smile with
delight. I felt encouraged, pampered. Was
it deliberately sent for me? I was racked with
thirst and both my water bottles were
empty. I asked for water and within a few
minutes I came across a small spring.

*To see a world
in a grain of sand
And a heaven
in a wild flower,
Hold infinity in the
palm of your hand
And eternity
in an hour.*

William Blake

Now well above the tree line, I started the long haul up Pinnacle Ridge, so named because it joins the Pinnacles I had walked over the previous week. It also had quite a few pinnacles of its own. They seemed to go on forever. Each one loomed up in front of me through the mist, each one required quite a climb, then down the other side of it and onto another. I felt the celestial cheering squad urging me on.

We're with you. We're proud of you.
You're doing so well.

I knew they were referring to my walking in harmony with them, not my physical struggle which seemed to be of little consequence in comparison.

I climbed throughout the afternoon. The cloud began to gather and the wind picked up, buffeting me, tugging at my clothes whenever I crossed an exposed section. As it increased I had to hang on lest I lose balance and be blown down. Eight peaks, nine – they seemed to go on forever. How many more?

This is the last one, this is the last peak.

I got to the top and saw that it was! "You are real, You don't lie, it is You! I believe – please, help my disbelief."

Only another hour or so and I'd be there, back in the safety and shelter of my mountain hut refuge. It was all gentle grades now,

Talent develops itself in solitude; character in the stream of life.

Johann Wolfgang von Goethe

but the wind steadily increased, heading up toward gale force, moaning around the ridges and peaks. Ordinarily I would have been very frightened to be out in these conditions, but today my fear was strangely absent.

It's not about you conquering your fear, it's about Me reducing it, so there is nothing to fear.

I bent into the gale, hugging the leeward sides of the ridge. Falling over, slipping on the greasy ground, and being blown off balance by the gusts I took many spills. Luckily, I fell mostly backward, crashing on my backpack which cushioned me from injury. Occasionally the wind chill got too much for me and to escape the freezing cold I'd stop for a while, huddling into the snow grass for shelter. Sufficiently revived, it was back again into the teeth of the gale. Pummeled by the wind and lashed by the rain, I struggled along the ridge line toward Arete. Finally I reached the hut, my shelter from the storm, my sanctuary. As I wearily closed the door, the howling fervor continued on, muffled by the four walls that now embraced me. Thank God I was home.

That night as I lay in bed, relishing my haven, the storm increased in intensity. It continued unabated for the next three days.

The wind in a man's face makes him wise.

John Ray

There was no way anyone was going to be out walking around in these atrocious conditions, so my solitude would not be under threat. But it had ceased to concern me. I was now open to receive whoever and whatever should happen along, sharing with them whatever I had. My rules had at last been beaten out of me. I realized my way of seeing events and the conclusions I leapt to were at best limited and often quite seriously flawed.

Sit loosely in the saddle of life.
Robert Louis Stevenson

The code I had constructed about what was right and wrong, about life, about solitude, about the way God worked, frequently hindered rather than enhanced my progress. I began to realize that so much of what comes my way may well be heaven sent. I had finally learned the lesson: to not judge events as good or bad, but to suspend judgement, keep the jury out, and just experience what's happening, deeply assured that all things turn out well for those who can openly receive the infinite compassion and love of The Source.

Interestingly enough, for the rest of my stay no one else came.

SIXTEEN

Cabin Fever

Day 20. Halfway. Snug and secure in my sleeping bag I listened to the storm furiously smashing into the hut. Tired from the last couple of days' exertions I welcomed this respite and was quite content to lie low for the time being.

What a different world I was now experiencing compared to the tranquillity of calm, fine days. The contrast gave meaning – to weather the storm is to enjoy the calm even more so. If every day boasted a perfect sunrise, calm blue skies and stunning sunsets, how blasé I'd get. Whereas, after three days of subzero gales, driving rain and sleet, a calm day seems doubly beautiful. Without clouds you can't have a sunset.

If we had no winter, the spring would not be so pleasant; if we had not sometimes taste of adversity, prosperity would not be so welcome.

Anne Bradstreet

(Could this also be true for my spiritual and emotional life?)

As I ran the recent events of my soul journey around in my head I seemed to keep bumping into the "mistakes." Dwelling inordinately on them I began to register them as failings rather than as great learning experiences.

You're very hard on yourself.

The storm continued unabated for the next two days. I had become a virtual prisoner inside the hut and I began to get bored. For some reason my thoughts and communications didn't seem to be going above the ceiling. I was plagued with "bees," I even smacked my head a few times trying to make them stop so I could concentrate on other more "pure" thoughts. But it made little difference; my mind leapt every which way.

All you have is this moment – enjoy it – don't plan, scheme, worry about what is or isn't to be, for in doing so you cheat yourself of what's here and now.

Dreams, plans, and then action. That's been my life. Always thinking ahead and scheming, how little time I've spent in the present. And here I was doing it again! Planning and scheming, rehearsing what was to be rather than being. I was annoyed. Here I was, on the mountain, my great opportunity to spend days just to be, to really go deep, to plumb the depths of the universe, but instead I had a head full of nonsense. For weeks I had spent many fruitless hours attempting to clear the "bees" when finally this

I don't need you to be a guru or a mystic. I have enough of those already – I just want you.

What a relief! What a breakthrough. I could just be me. I didn't have to change or become anything other than what I was, this alone is enough. It didn't matter that my head was a beehive – I could relax and be enjoyed. Again the messages of love and reassurance. There were no hurdles to jump over, no techniques to learn, no hard work to do. I could just celebrate what I enjoy. Be myself.

We are well pleased with you for being here. This alone is enough. I am not a harsh God. All I want is for you to know Me and enjoy Me, My love and My banquets. Be still and be blessed.

I must be a slow learner for soon I was asked

What are you looking forward to?

Many people tirade against the materialism and unspirituality of our age, but spirituality has been interpreted so narrowly that we do not recognize it when we meet it in ourselves and in others.

Gerard Hughes

> *We only confess our little faults to persuade people that we have no big ones.*
>
> François, Duc de la Rochefoucauld

> *Nine times out of ten, the coarse word is the word that condemns an evil and the refined word the word that excuses it.*
>
> G. K. Chesterton

I replied with a series of answers I hoped would please. They sounded plausible enough, but I somehow knew I wasn't giving the right replies. This was frustrating.

Are we having fun yet?

I ignored this. And on it went.

What are you afraid of?

I ran through all of my fears.

What are you afraid of?

I gave another shopping list of fears.

What are you afraid of?

I had run out. I had dug deep and still The Questioner asked. What the heck was going on?

Eventually it all got too much for me. Cooped up in the cabin for three days, thwarted in my efforts to please, baffled by not knowing what was going on, I broke. I screamed out, "What the _ _ _ _ do you want me to say! You brought me all the _ _ _ _ _ _ way up here, this is all your idea and now you've got me squirming like some insect on a pin! Do you get some sort of kick out of this? Is this how you get your supernatural jollies, teasing dumb humans like me? I'm trying to do the right thing here, and you stand away from me, keep me at arm's length. I'm hungry frustrated and _ _ _ _ _ _ bored and I don't know what you want me to say. Give us a break will ya… Help me, please!"

At last you've stopped pretending.
Now we've got some honesty here we
can really get stuck in.

I could almost feel the celestial sleeves being rolled up with delight, with pure joy that the façade had been broken through. All my life I'd tried to please people and here I was doing the same thing, trying to please God. To give the answers I thought were wanted. But God didn't give a toss about that, didn't want any of that sham. God just wanted me. Pure, unadulterated, vulnerable and weak me. That was who God ached to make contact with, not this mechanically programmed machine that would give a formula reply when a particular button was pressed. This beautiful God wanted me to share my heart's hurts, my heart's desires, my pain, my joy, my frustrations. Nothing less would do.

There is no surprise more magical than the surprise of being loved: it is God's finger on man's shoulder.

Charles Morgan

Stand alone with Me.

My Own One knew I was lying, knew that people-pleasing had become such an ingrained habit for me I no longer knew I was doing it. I had viewed life as some sort of exam where I did my best to give the "right" answers. But these weren't my answers, they were programmed replies, ones given so that I might get some sort of confidence vote from my peers. The Source

I'm looking for the face I had Before the world was made...

W. B. Yeats

wanted none of this, but instead wanted me to take off all the masks and see the face I had before the world was made. Only God knew what it looked like; it was the face God *always* saw. I had created all these other faces to avoid the pain of rejection, disappointment, and betrayal. I could almost hear the words, "Who said you had to do this? Whose rules are you playing by here? I didn't give you these rules." God ached for me to see this face and recognize it for the first time as being mine. I had seen myself through God's eyes and through that I had gotten a glimpse of who I really was. I was beautiful.

SEVENTEEN

How Strange It Is

I don't fit the picture of a hermit or a recluse. I am quite an extrovert; I love company and conversation and have a wide circle of friends, some of whom are very close. When I'm around, you can't help but notice me. "Rather loud" is a kind description (there are other less flattering ones). Talking has always been my forte. I'm never short of a word or a jibe and I like to be heard. So my claim that I was never lonely in the mountains may come as a bit of a surprise.

I was never lonely because I had with me at all times my best friend, father, lover, wise counselor, companion, confidant, rich old uncle, playmate, spiritual guide and master all rolled into one. The only differ-

Significant journeys cannot be accomplished without the nurture provided by a successful marriage or a successful society.

M. Scott Peck

ence was that none of these roles came with the usual human foibles, failings, and hidden agendas. This meant I had company different from any human companion. I might misunderstand what I was being told, but I knew I would never be misunderstood, for my deepest desires, worst fears and strongest longings were already intimately known.

All the sweetness of religion is conveyed to the world by the hands of storytellers and image-makers. Without their fictions the truths of religion would for the multitude be neither intelligible nor even apprehensible; and the prophets would prophesy and the teachers teach in vain.

George Bernard Shaw

So I found it strange that I was asked to tell my life story. If anyone knew it well, it was The Source. How bizarre, how odd! Nevertheless, I was intrigued, so I began. It developed into an ongoing conversation that continued over the next three to four days. To get me started or to keep me going I'd be asked questions:

Tell me about being a little boy. What did you enjoy most? When was the best time? What frightened you? What were your most treasured moments?

It was a wonderful exercise. I didn't have to consider whether or not I was boring my audience because The Master was so vitally interested in me. There were no accusations of being self-indulgent for it seemed The Source couldn't wait to hear all about me. I didn't have to hurry because someone else needed a turn, my Own One had all the time in the world and so did I. I didn't have to

justify, explain, analyze or come to any conclusions about the events of my life for I
knew God had been there too. And as I
spilled it all out to this most attentive of lis-
teners, I suspected I was somehow being
taught at the same time.

It was a joy to relate my earliest memories; the wonderful family I'd been born
into, how I had two parents that loved me
and an older brother and sister who enjoyed
me. In a way this was quite a surprise to me.
As an adult I had always claimed I'd had a
troubled early life. It now began to dawn on
me that this might not have been the case.
Not having to defend my behavior, but simply tell it, I was given permission to be gen-
erous, rather than bitter. Doing so in turn
released me to see how deeply and preciously my family loved me.

I was reminded of the times when I was
alone and close to God: as a youngster taking solitary walks down the creek and along
the beach; after school, on my own in the
rivers poaching trout; as a young man hitch-
hiking – rarely afraid – knowing I was Christ
on the road, never knowing where I would
rest my head. It was deliciously exciting,
trusting in God to guide me, to come
through for me.

Occasionally I'd be interrupted with a

*My faith is the grand
drama of my life. I'm
a believer, so I sing
words of God to those
who have no faith. I
give bird songs to
those who dwell in
cities and have never
heard them, make
rhythms for those
who know only
military marches or
jazz, and paint
colours for those who
see none.*

Olivier Messiaen

question, usually when I was offering up one of my distorted versions of the truth. Sometimes a question would be repeated again and again. One in particular continued for hours.

And what else did you enjoy about your first year at university

I had always claimed I made no friends there, that I was miserable, that I felt like an outsider, that I was excluded because I had gone to a public school and most others had been privately educated.

And what else did you enjoy about your first year at university?

I ran through the joy of learning, the start of friendships that have lasted a lifetime, an introduction to peace issues and justice, a love of literature, the poems of T. S. Eliot, an understanding of what motivates humans.

And what else did you enjoy about your first year at university?

I enjoyed the thrill of being part of something, of being different, of having long hair and being a rebel.

And what else did you enjoy about your first year at university?

This was getting annoying. I had run out of answers but as I dug deeper and continued to name the things I enjoyed, a differ-

The human heart dares not stay away too long from that which hurt it most. There is a return journey to anguish that few of us are released from making.

Lillian Smith

ent picture began to emerge. Out tumbled the scared, frightened little boy who had tried so hard to be brave and clever. I saw how in his fragility and insecurity he had selected a lineup of opponents, attacking them before they attacked him, and when they retaliated, as those under siege always do, they inevitably fulfilled his worst expectations. Viewed through what I had enjoyed, I began to realize what a tremendous opportunity it was to have been immersed in such a rich and exciting learning environment. How fortunate I was.

And so it continued, the gentle probing, the repeated questions that clarified, on and on through the years, until I came back to the mountain where I currently was. Like the Ancient Mariner, I had told my story to the wedding guest and now, for once in my life, I had nothing more to say. I was left with something I'd never expected when I'd begun my story all those days ago. In telling it like this, I ended up aware and deeply affected by how loved I was. So many people had touched me along my journey, been kind, done me favors, affirmed me, loved me, forgiven me, paid me, taught me, tended me, befriended me. So much generosity, so much tenderness, so much love!

This is the truth. Know it to be true.

You are much loved, if only you knew how much.

The next day I was asked to introduce Christine. Again, The Source listened totally, exceptionally interested in what I had to say as if everything I said was new and previously unknown. I talked about Christine in the same way I would to a favorite aunt who lived in a far-off country, but who was too old to travel and meet her. I acquainted The Source with who she is, what she likes, dislikes, her skills, attributes, things she enjoys doing, what she's good at, what she'd like to be good at, those she admires, her interests, what sort of person she is, what I liked about her. I talked, not about my frustrations, disappointments and complaints, but about who she was and the times we'd enjoyed together. It took all day and at the end of it I was stunned by how profoundly and deeply I loved her. Just as when I discovered the love others had for me, this time I was staggered by the love I had for her.

And so it went on. I introduced my sons, my parents, my brother and sister, my friends, relatives, acquaintances, anyone I could think of. At the end I became aware, not only of how much I love them but how much they are loved by the One I'd introduced them to. It was a reservoir

The sum which two married people owe to one another defies calculation. It is an infinite debt, which can only be discharged through all eternity.

Johann Wolfgang von Goethe

Chains do not hold a marriage together. It is threads, hundreds of tiny threads which sew people together through the years. That is what makes a marriage last – more than passion or even sex!

Simone Signoret

I'd hardly tapped.

I learned so much from this activity. When I simply tell or hear a story I am so much more open to discovering truth than when I'm involved in analyzing, justifying or explaining. Verdicts and conclusions, whether they be mine or someone else's, seem to invite me to be critical. Stories or retellings invite me to listen, to be heard, to learn and to discover.

The shortest distance between a human being and Truth is a story.

Anthony de Mello

EIGHTEEN

On the Mountain

The morning after the storm blew over I emerged from the hut into a different world. It was pay-back time for the mountains. Freed from days of stoically withstanding the pounding, buffeting and drenching, they now unleashed their soaked-up suffering. All around, the gullies and valleys echoed to a solid roar, a cascading crescendo of dozens of waterfalls spewing their overload downward.

Water was pouring from every orifice, oozing from every crack. From the tinkling of nearby tiny rivulets to the tumbling, gushing, rushing of swollen streams, the highlands were disgorging their burden. As if in competition to see who could purge

True solitude is a din of birdsong, seething leaves, whirling colours, or a clamor of tracks in the snow.

Edward Hoagland

their load first, every bluff, cliff and precipice had sprung a thousand leaks.

I didn't know it at the time, but I was about to be treated to a spell of clear, cloudless weather that would last for five days. Most of this time I spent on the summit. It was quite flat with a few groups of rocks I could perch on. There, surrounded by an unimpeded 360-degree view, I stood and sat on my heartland. But not only my heartland, this was the very heart of the whole mountain range. I had only just discovered from the map that this peak, Arete, the one I had been irresistibly drawn to for all these years, was the starting point of five of the seven major rivers of the range. No wonder I was here! This was where the source and soul of the mountains resided, its core, its lifeblood, its essence, the start of so many beginnings, my place to be.[1]

Supported by my rock throne I had a grandstand view, and there, as the days slipped by, I watched the daily routines, learned the moods of the mountains – alternately bathed in light, shadow and dark, now and then cloaked in mist. Occasionally the wind would caress them, combing the snow grass like fields of wheat. At

The only business of the head in the world is to bow a ceaseless obeisance to the heart.

W. B. Yeats

[1] I later learned the Maori (New Zealand's indigenous people) name for Arete is *Hanga-o-hia-tangata*, "the place that caused surprise to man" - how appropriate!

other times it was so still, so breathless, frag-
ile-winged dragonflies could hover undisturbed. It was full, splendid, astounding,
and all so perfect.

I saw things I would have missed were I
just passing by. The mountain itself is quite
irregular in shape so it was with some incredulity that I noticed in the early morning a perfect pyramid-shaped shadow was
being cast onto the glaciated valley below.
Then, when the late afternoon sun came
upon it, the valley behind me also received
another perfect pyramid-shaped shadow –
quite extraordinary.

Sometimes it was hard to believe I
wasn't the only living soul in the world, especially when the valleys below were completely cloud covered, leaving me basking
in brilliant sunshine. Those lower down
would be experiencing a dull day. It was the
same day, the same place, but I was having
a totally different experience of it. I'm sure
it was the same for those below when they
had fine days and I was in cloud.

On a few late afternoons, clouds formed
in front of me for no apparent reason. At
other times I'd see them relentlessly creep
their way up from the broad coastal plains.
Starting 1500 meters below, they'd take
hours, inexorably rolling toward me like

The most beautiful emotion we can experience is the mystical. It is the power of all true art and science. He to whom this emotion is a stranger, who can no longer wonder and stand rapt in awe, is as good as dead.

Albert Einstein

Touched by grace, highly unlikely beneficial events happen to us all the time, quietly, knock-ing on the door of our awareness no more dramatically than the beetle gently tapping on the windowpane.

M. Scott Peck

huge white slugs, hugging the valley floors, lying low until reaching the headwaters and spilling over the lowest pass into the next valley on a never-ceasing search to smother all with an enormous cotton wool blanket.

One Saturday, I experienced one of the most beautiful days ever.

Finally freed of my concern to be left alone, I eagerly waited on top of the mountain to share this glorious day with the climbers I was certain would soon arrive. It was such a rare day I was convinced there would be quite a few, especially considering the disparaging comments in the log book about the appallingly bad weather usually encountered up here. "Blowing a gale, cloudy and miserable." "Too windy on tops – heading down to the valley." "Freezing cold, waist-deep snow, too hard to go on – typical bloody weather," and many other equally sour remarks.

I waited and watched, drinking in the incredible views. The islands in the royal blue sea sparkled as the huge expanse of ocean disappeared toward the horizon. Everything was so cloud free and pure, I knew it didn't get any better than this. But no one came.

The next day, Sunday, I was up at sunrise, spellbound, mesmerized by the beauty.

Faith is an excitement and an enthusiasm: it is a condition of intellectual magnificence to which we must cling as to a treasure, and not squander on our way through life in the small coin of empty words, or in exact and priggish argument.

George Sand

Sometimes I stood like a human sundial, scanning the everchanging high cloud patterns, identifying the light changes on the peaks I'd walked over as a young man and wondering, always wondering. Finally came the three-hour-long twilight, dusk, then sunset was complete and left me with the crystal clear fairyland twinkling lights of the towns spread far and wide below me. Simply magic. Two stunningly glorious calm, clear days in a row. But no one came.

Lost, yesterday, somewhere between sunrise and sunset, two golden hours, each set with sixty diamond minutes. No reward is offered, for they are gone forever.

Horace Mann

I began to understand Christ's parable of the banquet. This weekend an amazingly majestic visual banquet had been thrown with very few taking up the invitation to feast. The Source had been stood up. It no doubt happens all the time. The banquets of colossal beauty are spread out for all to enjoy, but no one comes.

How often I've looked up at mountains on days such as these and wished myself there, but didn't go. I now know I was not alone in my wish. The One who loves me outrageously must have ached to lavish these feasts upon me.

But I'd been too busy to attend or I felt I didn't have a right to be there because I had people to see, kids to parent, friends to visit, money to earn, house renovations to complete, other chores to perform. If I had spent

We are ashamed to seem evasive in the presence of a straightforward man, cowardly in the presence of a brave one, gross in the eyes of a refined one, and so on. We always imagine, and in imagining share, the judgments of the other mind.

Charles Horton Cooley

Beauty is one of the rare things that do not lead to doubt of God.

Jean Anouilh

too much time in the mountains, the haranguing Greek chorus of accusations in my head would have told me, "You're irresponsible, lazy. What have you to show for this time you're wasting?" But whose voice was I hearing?

One morning when awakened, I looked out the hut door, and there again was the breathless scene that had touched me all those years ago: the V-shaped pass with a layer of beautiful fluffy pure white cloud stretched across it, the radiant sun just starting to peak over the top. Again I was overwhelmed. It seemed put there just for me. I immediately headed for the summit. It was another stunningly beautiful day. I sat there in the subzero temperatures until the sun was directly overhead. By this time I was hungry and also aware that sitting in the snow had chilled my feet. I figured I'd seen the best of the day so I started to walk back down to the hut for a bite to eat and a change of scenery. As I walked this conversation started:

Where are you going?

Back down to the hut.

Why?

I've got cold feet, I'm bored and a bit hungry.

How many times have you turned

and walked away from me
because you had "cold feet," were
"hungry" or "bored"?

Ouch. I continued for a few more steps
while this sunk in and then, without breaking stride, turned right around and went
back onto the top. The next six hours were
stupendous.

This was one of the times I responded
fairly quickly, but there were many other
times I didn't. It was easy when the invitations coincided with what I wanted to do, but
when they required a bit of effort, were potentially uncomfortable, or deviated from
what I had in mind, I'd have to be invited repeatedly before I'd act, if at all.

It's a bit like when I'm lying in bed
slightly chilled. I know that an extra blanket is what's needed to warm me up, but that
means getting out of bed to get it, and getting cold in the process. So I lie there, unable to go to sleep because I'm cold, yet reluctant to take that one step necessary for
warmth. Eventually I either drift off into a
chilly listless half sleep, dozing on and off
all night, or I take a deep breath, brave the
minute or two of freezing and get the blanket. Later as I lie there warm and content I
wonder why on earth I didn't do it sooner!

I responded in a similar way to the in-

It may be that each
individual conscious-
ness is a brain cell in
a universal mind.

Sir James Jeans

ner voice. I deferred the calls without fully understanding why. Perhaps it is part of being human? But I try now to ask for strength to do the things which are difficult and to forgive myself when I fail. It doesn't always work, but somehow I have no doubt the invitations will never be withdrawn. They may be reworded and come in a different shape but in the same way we're destined to repeat life's lessons until we learn them, they will come round again. The spiritual path is a gentle one; the world's way is harder.

Love cures people, the ones who receive love and the ones who give it too.

Karl A. Menninger

During the first few days on the mountain I kept rushing to the summit to see how the view was on the other side. I hated the thought of missing out on any majestic sights. I kept doing this for a few days before the thought occurred to me, "What exactly am I missing out on? Haven't I been woken at exactly the right time on every occasion it was important? Did I ever miss out when I obeyed? Wasn't the timing absolutely perfect when I responded to the inner voice? Weren't things appalling when I did it on my own strength? How can I 'miss out' if I am doing exactly what I am asked to do?"

If I trust, it will be perfect, in tune, complete and whole. By contrast, if I take charge or listen to the chorus of accusations, I will always be out of sync. I will exhaust myself on a vicious circle of trying to keep up with what I might be missing, then swallowing the bitter pills of jealousy and remorse when I see that I have indeed "missed out." For in seeking not to miss out, I inevitably find I have. I am beginning to suspect the whole notion of missing out is really envy. By accepting and totally trusting in "The Way," I discovered I'd identified one of the major monkeys on my back. Freed from the fear of missing out, life seemed far simpler.

Anxiety is the great modern plague. But faith can cure it.

Smiley Blanton

Mid-afternoon one calm, clear day, I was sitting outside the hut gazing toward the distant lowland valleys. I thought of getting up and moving on when once again a song invited me to stay a while with my Own One. I remained, and a few minutes later a flock of small birds flew past. I'd often seen these birds around the mountain tops. They usually hung out in pairs or small groups – never alone. However, on this day, moments after the main flock had passed, a solitary bird flew by chirping for all it was worth, desperately trying to catch up with the others. As it drew parallel to me, about 20 meters away, what I thought was a large boulder hit it in mid-flight!

It was so sudden and so unexpected that

I thought someone must have dropped a rock on the poor thing. In the split second that followed I was about to look up to see who could throw with such accuracy, when I heard shrill chirping off to my left. There, about 40 meters away, the huge wings of a bird of prey were just spreading out, lifting its hapless victim, now firmly clasped in its claws, up and away.

It was all over in seconds but the memory of it is so clear. What an amazing feat of nature I had just witnessed! New Zealand falcons are an endangered species. Sightings of them are extremely rare, let alone close-up views of their spectacular hunting methods.

What are you looking forward to?

A physical visitation would be nice.

You have no idea what you are asking for.

One evening when there was no sunset, just an amazing array of skies, I recalled one of my most precious memories. The trust that a small child places in me, especially when I'm their dad, is one of the most beautiful, priceless experiences I've had. When that little body raises its arms to be held it knows it will be safe. When they fall asleep on me having absolute faith that I'll put them to bed and still love them in the morn-

> *The individual who has experienced solitude will not easily become a victim of mass suggestion.*
>
> Albert Einstein

> *It is impossible to repent of love, the sin of love does not exist.*
>
> Muriel Spark

ing – it's heaven on a stick. So total is their trust it's almost overwhelming. How preciously and delicately I always treated this confidence, for to betray it would be a monstrous crime.

If I feel this, how much more must The Almighty feel about us, God's human adult children? Imagine The Creator's joy when an adult, full of logic, fear and self-will, turns from what they know and offers their total trust? If we, who are mere mortals, are touched so much by our children's trust, how much more will the Eternal Presence value ours? How could God ever betray it? Maybe this is how our souls magnify the Lord?

Another wonderful day. Not a sound, total stillness with only the occasional gentle breeze brushing against my cheek. I sat and gaped at the arrayed splendor in front of me, set out like some visual smorgasbord. I could take my fill of whatever scene titillated my appetite. One particular valley looked as if it had been scooped out by a spatula drawn through margarine. Being very deep, it received only a few hours sunlight and as the day progressed I watched the shadows cast by the nearby mountains once again drop their dark curtains across the valley.

God is beauty.
St. Francis of Assisi

This then is salvation: When we marvel at the beauty of created things and praise their beautiful creator.

Meister Eckhart

I looked off into the mid-distance where another set of snow capped peaks were blasted by full sunlight, sparkling in such a way to appear as if dancing, but they too were eventually bathed in shadow as the sun moved on. Cocooned and mesmerized by such visual treats, and now in what I considered to be a suitably receptive mood, I cheekily put up a challenge.

Okay, God, talk to me about stuff.

I prefer to let my art speak for itself!

Touché!

Day 27. It was time to review more of the rules I had made for myself regarding solitude. I started making a few jottings in an old disused notebook I found in the hut. It was the first thing I had written for nearly a month. It was now right to write. I was slowly learning to listen, to glide and move upon the gentle rhythms of grace. I was learning that things must happen in their own time. In the past I'd all too often find myself pleading for things to hurry up and happen. The inner voice had guided me.

You can't have what you ask for. It's like saying "I want it to be midday (zap), no dusk(zap), no dawn (zap)." Things have their own natural order and seasons, learn to flow within these.

The blues and deep greens of the early mornings gave way to the golds and greens of the midday sun on the snow grass and leatherwood below me; the splashes of white snow stoodout starkly from the black cold rocks; the shadowed sausages of rolling hills darkened as the sun dipped over them, and dissolved into the deep purples, oranges and furnace reds of sundown – a never ending kaleidoscope of color.

Nothing in all creation is so God-like as stillness
Meister Eckhart

Coming and going. Round and round. Over and over. So simple. So peaceful. These, the small events, slowly accumulated to reveal the bigger picture. I considered that maybe in our lives, too, the small events are just as important as the big ones. Each word we utter, thought we create, and action we undertake is perhaps as crucial to the big picture as "major" decisions like marriage, moving house, changing jobs or having kids. Yet so often we rank our words and deeds into "important" or "insignificant" and act accordingly. But perhaps it's the long-term accumulated total of all our actions that is most telling? The little things we do that cement friendships, strengthen bonds, and lay the foundations for future happiness.

A man is a method, a progressive arrangement; a selecting principle, gathering his like unto him wherever he goes. What you are becomes you.
Ralph Waldo Emerson

Like snowflakes: on their own, each one is "insignificant," but together they have a profound impact. Gently settling on top of one another, their combined weight compresses the lower layers into ice. Months and years of this create thousands of tonnes of ice, a glacier that flows downward carving through mountains as if they were cheese.

The months and years of our thoughts, words, and deeds do the same to the mountains we choose to live on.

NINETEEN

Rats, Fire and Snow

I wasn't completely alone in my hut. I had the company of a small rodent. "Rattles," I named her, for that was what she did. An hour or two after I'd gone to bed, she'd emerge from the darkness and start chewing on something, waking me up in the process. Then a game would start that went something like this: I thumped the wall which scared her enough to stop chewing for a while, then when she thought enough time had elapsed for the dozy human to be asleep again (which he usually was), she'd recommence chewing, and so on we'd go, seesawing through the night until dawn when she'd retire to wherever it was she spent the daylight hours.

The first night, before I was aware of her presence, she'd actually got into my backpack and helped herself to a few rolled oats. From then on, each evening I hung my backpack from a nail hammered into one of the rafters. That stopped her little red wagon for a while, but she soon enough found something else to chew on. I couldn't help admiring her perseverance. To survive up there for months at a time in subzero temperatures was nothing short of miraculous. However, my admiration for her decreased as she became bolder and bolder. One night I decided she'd gone too far when I caught her in my flashlight beam. She just looked at me as if to say, "Yeah, what?" then nonchalantly walked off, continuing with her chewing. "Right," I thought, "that's it!"

I didn't have the heart to kill her for she had as much right to be there as I did, but I definitely wanted her gone. So I hatched a plan to spring her from her daytime quarters. I assumed she was in the darkest corner of the hut where I'd put the junk from the first day's tidy up. I started by creating a nice dark tunnel leading directly from the junk pile to the door. For this I used the black plastic from the cooking bench. Then I completely gutted the hut, placing outside everything that wasn't attached. My scheme

I know not what you believe of God, but I believe He gave yearnings and longings to be filled, and that He did not mean all our time should be devoted to feeding and clothing the body.

Lucy Stone

ran something like this: with nowhere else to run and hide, Rattles would head down the dark tunnel encouraged by much wild noise and stamping from myself and by the time she realized where she was I'd have shut the door and *voilà*, no more rodent!

I poised myself, ready to deliver the frightening noise. Cautiously, I removed the last piece of junk. No rat! Damn and double damn! Where the hell was she? The only thing I hadn't removed from the whole hut was one of the mattresses. So that's where she was! I couldn't think of any way to flush her out of there so, congratulating her on winning yet another round, I resigned myself to limiting her nighttime activities. Each evening as I retired, as well as suspending my backpack, I also suspended the mattress from the ceiling. The poor little blighter, she must have done it hard for about five days, but eventually her patience was rewarded. One night when I was preoccupied with other thoughts I neglected to string things up and the next morning I discovered she'd hit the jackpot, scoring a direct hit on my rolled oats and milk powder! What an amazing example of patience and cunning. As far as I know she's still there. I wish her well.

Once again I found myself storm-bound. This one was a real doozey, with four

If we didn't live venturously, plucking the wild goat by the beard, and trembling over precipices, we should never be depressed, I've no doubt; but already should be faded, fatalistic and aged.

Virginia Woolf

days of gut-wrenching, wild, hammering gales. During the first two nights the door was repeatedly blown open, so in the end I lashed it shut. It was hard to believe there wasn't some malevolent force out there trying to get in and hammer me to death as the hut was thumped over and over again by an incredible pounding. There I was with the hatches thoroughly bolted down, the rain falling so hard and in such volume I felt like I was trapped in one of those old movie squall scenes where fire hoses and wind machines are used to simulate a storm. I'd sealed the windows with soap to lessen the amount of water coming through. Now, with the wind behind it, the rain was forced through this soap caulking, producing a frothing mass of bubbles.

It was bitterly cold. Lying in my top-grade sleeping bag I still had all my clothes on, five layers on my top half, three on the bottom – all thermal polypropylene. My neck warmer and hat were also permanently on. Some mornings I discovered the water in my water bottle was frozen, as was the hut floor. This proved to be quite a bonus for it meant I could scrape the rough ice off the floor with the spade I found in the hut, thus removing much of the damp that had soaked into it.

Mountains are to the rest of the body of the earth, what violent muscular action is to the body of man. The muscles and tendons of its anatomy are, in the mountain, brought out with force and convulsive energy, full of expression, passion, and strength.

John Ruskin

On Day 32 I noted in my journal: "My poor toes, they seem to be bearing the brunt of all this." My thick socks tended to reduce the circulation to my feet so I kept only one layer of socks on when in and around the hut. At this stage I was unaware that these were the first signs something serious was happening.

I want to get closer to you over the next few days.

As I lay there and mused, I asked repeatedly what I should do to get closer. I kept getting the same message.

Listen to the wind.

I'd do this for a while and then drift off onto other thoughts, then return to where I was and what should I be doing.

Listen to the wind.

Again I'd try for a while, quite bewildered about what I was or wasn't supposed to conclude from the wind. The great thing was it didn't bother me too much. If I was supposed to get some deeper meaning, it would all be revealed eventually. Just as with the Statue of Sorrows, when my eyes were ready to see they would.

Listen to the wind.

Eventually it occurred to me that the wind groaning, roaring and moaning around the hut sounded exactly like I was

The opposite of love is not hate, it's indifference. The opposite of art is not ugliness, it's indifference. The opposite of faith is not heresy, it's indifference. And the opposite of life is not death, it's indifference.

Elie Wiesel

in the middle of a blast furnace. When smelting steel, occasionally they put a lance into the heart of the furnace and inject pure oxygen into it. When this happens it's hard to believe the furnace isn't alive. The roar is incredible, as if someone had put a barbed lance into the dragon's lair, pierced its skin, and then injected it with a painful poison. There's an explosion of tormented agony. It sounds terrifying, but it's a necessary part of the steel-refining process... Bingo! I was being purified by the storm. Earlier I'd been singing a song *Refiner's Fire*, and now it was happening.

As if I were experiencing some gigantic celestial radiation treatment, I lay in my small cell and opened myself up to be purged and cleansed. I asked that the cancers of guilt, greed, envy, fear, pain, sorrow, regret, people-pleasing, lust, cruelty, self-hate, anger and hardheartedness be taken away from me and be replaced by love, pure golden love, purifying my heart, restoring my soul. For the rest of the storm days I lay back, relishing the refining process. I no longer cared that I was confined to quarters by the storm; in fact it seemed quite appropriate. I could almost imagine the sign on the hut door saying, DO NOT ENTER. REFINING PROCESS IN OPERATION.

It needs leisure to think things out; it needs leisure to mature. People in a hurry cannot think, cannot grow, nor can they decay. They are preserved in a state of perpetual puerility.

Eric Hoffer

The beauty of this particular refining process was that I didn't have to do anything except receive it. I couldn't go anywhere even if I'd wanted to. I was stuck there, completely safe, while white-winged technicians off in another room dialed in the appropriate dosage to ensure the purification process effected a cure.

Soon silence will have passed into legend. Man has turned his back on silence.

Jean Arp

Outside, the power of the storm was awesome. Gusting this way and that, twisting and turning, hell-bent on "getting there," it writhed and thrashed about like some half-crazed beast tormented by pain. At one stage, the entire south wall of the hut bulged inward under the staggering power of the wind. The refining process was certainly violent. Finally, just before dawn on the sixth day, it ceased.

What a contrast! I opened the door to be met by a fantastic fairyland of pure white. A stunning wrapping of snow had been dumped over everything, covering all the dark ugly patches, leaving all a pristine virginal white. Whereas before I could distinguish pretty or unsightly, charming or displeasing, now it was impossible to differentiate. The princes and paupers of scenery had all been rendered equally beautiful by nature's purest of clothes. The snow's sound-insulating effect soaked up and

God is voluptuous and delicious.

Meister Eckhart

muffled all noise. As if in respectful awe, all was hushed, offering up an appropriate reverence. I, too, crept about not wishing to disturb the silence.

The brutality of the storm had metamorphosed to become the beauty of the calm. It seemed the tougher the refining process, the more dramatic the results. It was as if the forces of darkness and death that did furious battle here for days had been vanquished by the good guys – a total transformation from hell to heaven.

Being on the mountain top I could relate to those who stand out in the human world. Leaders and pathfinders get wonderful views and magnificent sunsets, but when the storms hit there is no shelter. They're fully exposed and vulnerable, shielded only by whatever protective clothing they have with them. Those who stay in the valleys will never be exposed to the extremes of the storms, but neither will they experience the stunning sunsets and grand views.

One is not idle because one is absorbed. There is both visible and invisible labour. To contemplate is to toil, to think is to do. The crossed arms work, the clasped hands act. The eyes upturned to Heaven are an act of creation.

Victor Hugo

It was Day 35 and it seemed the scene was now set for a perfect "final act" – a cosmic curtain call, The Source's one final fling to show me perfect art, God's permanent work in progress. The mountain panorama was breathtaking. A clear, brilliant blue sky set off the white-capped peaks and I was the only one, the only one for God knows how far to be drinking all this in! Dare I believe this was for me?

The snow was perfect, not so deep as to make walking difficult but deep enough to spectacularly coat everything. It was just what I prayed, wished and hoped for – so bright so clear, I was truly blessed.

You can go up and have a look if you like.

What type of inner voice command is that? If "I like"? Then I realized it was the soft invitation of a lover. I walked up to the summit and was surprised at how warm and comfy the snow was. On the summit I simply didn't have the words to describe what I could see. Snowcapped mountains stretching dozens of kilometers in both directions – superb, stunning, almost surreal. My only response was to sing.

Have I told you lately that I love you?
Fill me up from your loving cup.
Give me my rapture today.

© Van Morrison

Music expresses what we cannot put into words and that which cannot remain silent.

Victor Hugo

A deluge of song lines tumbled out as I clumsily tried to express my total awe and appreciation: *Day by Day* from *Godspell*, Dolly Parton and Kenny Roger's *Islands in the Stream*, Frank Ifield's *I Love You Be-*

cause, climaxing with *Amazing Grace* sung full gusto.

Amazing grace
How sweet the sound
That saved a wretch like me
I once was lost
But now am found
Was blind
But now I see.

As I sang, my Own One turned the songs around and sang them back to me! As if providing the banquet wasn't enough, God wanted to tell me how much I was loved for simply being there, for just for turning up!

That evening, due to a band of cloud that hovered above the horizon, I was treated not to one glorious sunset, but two! After the last shreds of red dissolved, I retraced my footsteps in the snow, the moon lighting my path so I could see my way without a light. After dinner, I danced outside the hut, stamping my feet as I sang *Moondance*, *Blue Moon* and any other song with moon in it, including *Silent Night* and other snowy Christmas carols.

I was intoxicated. I was in love with life, God, the universe, everything. And all around me seemed to know it too. The moonlit dress circle of mountains, like wise elders, beamed back their unperturbed si-

Music is well said to be the speech of angels; in fact, nothing among the utterances allowed to man is felt to be so divine. It brings us near to the infinite.

Thomas Carlyle

There is something haunting in the light of the moon; it has all the dispassionateness of a disembodied soul, and something of its inconceivable mystery.

Joseph Conrad

lence. They had seen it all millions of times before, so what was all the fuss about? But secretly I knew when they were young, they too had danced to this tune and if pressed, would love to do so again.

I lingered, drinking it all in, using my body to express what words could not. Reluctant to let this moment pass, somehow trying to preserve the fervor of erupting emotions, I stayed well into the night. It had been a perfect day with a perfect God in a perfect place. I declared I didn't want to be anywhere else with anybody else doing anything else. This was it, heaven on earth. Finally I went to bed, drifting into an almost postcoital sleep, so enraptured was I.

Man is to be found in reason, God in the passions.

G. C. Lichtenberg

But while my inner journey was at an all-time high, my outer physical journey had taken a massive plunge. Carried away by all that was laid out before me I had stayed too long in the snow.

TWENTY

Cold Feet

In my youth I had happily tramped many hours through snow, my feet usually going numb and staying that way all day. However, they always thawed out overnight, so I was quite unconcerned when my feet went numb this time. I had top quality thermal clothing and brilliantly insulating storm gear. Even so, I had taken extra precautions such as only wearing dry socks and drying my boots at every opportunity. When sitting in the snow on top of the mountain, I would change out of my circulation restricting boots, replace them with sneakers and warm socks, then place my legs and feet in a big plastic rubbish bag thoroughly insulating them from the cold.

Perfect courage means doing unwitnessed what we would be capable of with the world looking on.

François, Duc de la Rochefoucauld

But during the previous night's snow dancing rapture I had ignored my cold feet and
left my boots on too long. The next morning I woke up expecting my feet to be back
to normal, to have fully regained all feeling,
but they were still numb, they hadn't thawed
out. At first I wasn't all that perturbed. I
heated up some water and put it in my plastic drink bottle, then used this as a rudimen-
tary hot water-bottle. I left it on my toes all
day. The small toes regained feeling, and
they all felt warm to the touch, but the big
toes were still numb. I could stick a needle
right into them and feel nothing. I knew
they had been frostbitten. What I didn't
know was how badly, and what I should do
about it. I felt sick in the stomach, that
dreadful realization that you've made a mistake, a miscalculation, and nothing you do
can change the way things are.

*Man's extremity is
God's opportunity.*

John Flavel

All I knew about frostbite was your flesh
died, went black, turned gangrenous, and
then you had the affected limb amputated.
My mind immediately conjured up scenes
of operating theaters, surgeons sharpening
their scalpels like butchers preparing to
pare the back steaks off a carcass.

I'd read books about climbers who had
suffered frostbite and I'd also made a film
about two men who'd had their frostbitten

feet amputated just below the knee. It is not a pleasant process and entails years of rehabilitation, not to mention the excruciating pain and suffering. My eldest son had accidentally chopped the top off his finger a few years before and I well remember not only the agony he went through after his amputation, but also the impact on those who loved him. It was all very well for me to go and sit on the mountain and get the pleasure, but how fair was it to my wife and family to bring them back years of pain?

This was the downside of solitude. With no one to put on a brave face for, I found myself quickly derailed into fear and panic. Having no other person to consult, I only had what I knew. I couldn't get a second opinion, couldn't get reassurance or comfort, I was totally and absolutely alone – or was I? What of my inner voice, what did it have to say about all this?

"Are my toes okay? Reassure me here, I'm worried to the quick. I don't want to lose my toes. I'll put up with numb feet for the rest of my life as long as they don't get the chop!"

It's happening, wait. Trust, you did have frostbite but we're fixing it. We're getting somewhere with what you are doing.

Nothing gives a fearful man more courage than another's fear.

Umberto Eco

Doubt is the oxygen that feeds the candle of faith.

Peter Cameron

(I was massaging and keeping the hot, drinking-water bottle on them.)

Check your other toes. Notice how the tips of them don't feel the pinprick either? They'll be numb for a few weeks but they're going to be all right. Trust, have faith."

"I believe, please help my disbelief."

The bones in my big toes felt as if they'd been replaced by cold stainless steel. Just sitting there and dwelling on it was hard. About midmorning it got too hard to be brave. I broke, I had to do something. I decided I wanted off this mountain. I was getting out of there. The weather was reasonable. So, without any reference to the inner voice I hurriedly packed my backpack, made a final check of the hut, and started to head out the door when,

Won't you stay a while with your own one?

I sat outside the hut for a while and waited for further instructions. Eventually

Unpack your bag, we're staying put today. There's great danger if you leave now.

Somehow I got myself together enough to unpack. After all, it had been called right every other time and this certainly sounded like the right voice; I didn't think I was be-

People who are born even-tempered, placid and untroubled – secure from violent passions or temptations to evil – those who have never needed to struggle all night with the Angel to emerge lame but victorious at dawn, never become great saints.

Eva le Gallienne

ing deceived. After the earlier incident where I'd jammed my flashlight in my pocket, I recalled how easily spooked and panicked I could become. So I heeded the warning and unpacked. But I wasn't happy. My habit in times of crisis is not just to sit there, but to do something. Doing something makes me feel better. Whether it's effective or not is irrelevant; it's the doing that counts. Maybe The Source knew this, because I was bidden to get on with the chores, tidy up and bury my feces. Some good old dirty stuff to bring me back to earth and some "doing" to calm me down.

And then the thought police started in. What if this delay meant I might miss out on a blood thinning drug that could save my toes? "If only we'd caught it in time. Why did you stay when you could have got help?" Or alternatively "Why did you pull out? Where is your faith? Why were you so afraid? Didn't your God come through for you?" All these accusations. I don't think there was one I didn't consider.

He's sure got you wound up on this one hasn't he?"
Are my toes okay?
Sure, they've been like this for three weeks, if frostbitten they'd be black by now.

Saintliness is also a temptation.
Jean Anouilh

*Courage is the price
that Life exacts for
granting peace, the
soul that knows it not,
knows no release from
little things; knows
not the livid loneliness
of fear, nor mountain
heights where bitter
joy can hear the sound
of wings.*

Amelia Earhart

*Religion is love; in no
case is it logic.*

Beatrice Potter Webb

What do I do?

Stay with me.

So many different voices. Which one was the right one? So many different thoughts, so much panic, so much worry, so much anxiety. What should I do? I counted the next 36 hours as among the worst I had ever lived. This was faith, real faith. Scared, frightened, alone, and totally panicked, I alternated between terror and reassurance. I didn't sleep at all but just kept boiling water in the vain hope a miracle would happen and my toes would return to normal. I prayed and begged and raved and ranted.

"I'm so scared. So frightened. Please, God, take away the numbness. A miracle, please." These were no cool, "at one with the universe," carefully considered prayers, but gut-wrenching beggings and pleadings. Tearful rages: "I am so vulnerable and afraid. Come through for me please!"

I had never had such a sustained period of absolute terror in all my life. It alternated with periods of calm reassurance where I knew it was all right, and I deeply believed. When I was in that state, I couldn't understand why at other times I was so panicked. But panic I did. When captured in those times of terror, I couldn't believe I had ever been so reassured and calm! How could I get back to those times of faith and solace?

One thing that definitely didn't work was logic. I "logiced" my brain out, amassing evidence for faith, pointing out the track record of The Source on this journey and others, reassuring myself of all the right signs, but it made not a scrap of difference. For inextricably bound up in the case for the defence was the case for the prosecution that seemed to amass more and more evidence that faith was akin to foolishness. No amount of logic seemed to stop full-blown fear.

I was now so worried I couldn't eat! How ironic. For days I'd been having pleasant thoughts about how and when I was going to eat my rations and now I couldn't face them. Ahead I faced another long night, my 36th evening alone. The dark night of the soul? I don't know, but somewhere during the blackness of that night I gave up, tuned out the voices in my head, both good and bad, and resorted back to me.

In the morning I took some action. I used my emergency radio and called up for a medical opinion on what was happening to my toes. In consultation with the base operator I decided to head down to the val-

The chains of habit are too weak to be felt until they are too strong to be broken.

Samuel Johnson

ley below where we would reassess the situation. Hopefully by then they would have had time to gather some information about frostbite. Just talking to someone else and doing something took away much of the panic and the terror, but I was still wound up with worry.

The only completely consistent people are the dead.
Aldous Huxley

The problem with leaving at this moment was that another storm had come in. It was now raining heavily and blowing a gale. I couldn't stand up against the wind (gusting at least 150 kilometers an hour) and so my planned route out over the mountain tops was far too dangerous. I'd have to bash my way down the stream that started below the hut. This would inevitably lead me into dangerous ravines, steep gorges and hectares of impenetrable leatherwood; but I considered that a far better alternative to sitting in the hut worrying.

TWENTY-ONE

Crash Landings

I engaged the old familiar will-power-crash-through mode and slithered and slid my way through the now melting snow into the headwaters of Arete stream. There began a hazardous trek downward that seriously risked my life. The rain had melted much of the snow thereby releasing all the stored up water from the previous week's storm. A month's subsistence rations now showed up in my body's distinct lack of energy. I didn't trust my sense of balance sufficiently to hop from boulder to boulder as I normally would, so I half walked, half slid along, using my hands and backside to balance on the cold slippery rocks.

    As I scrambled down the watercourse,

Obedience keeps the rules. Love knows when to break them.
Anthony de Mello

the stream soon turned into a river, then a swollen river, and then started running over waterfalls, pitching downward many meters into black, dank gorges and ravines. Engorged and swollen, the waterfalls would have been inspiring if they hadn't been such a dangerous obstacle in my dash to safety. The only way past each one was to climb up the bank above it, sidle along the top of the gorge walls using the leatherwood and other shrubs as a climbing frame, and climb back down into the riverbed only when well past the falls and the deep pools at the bottom. Some waterfalls and their gorges were a few meters high, others had sheer bluffs that required over 100 meters of upward thrashing.

We lie loudest when we lie to ourselves.

Eric Hoffer

Wet, tired, and anxious, covered in broken twigs and leaf litter, I drew on pure reserves of will power, mixed with fear, adrenalin, stubbornness and pride. Having made my decision to go it alone I thought it would compromise my integrity to now ask The Source to help me on my journey. I had made my bed, so it was up to me to lie in it. At least there was one good thing about tuning out the spiritual channel – the accuser was also off air. I continued along like this in spiritual neutral for hours, thrashing and crashing until the inevitable happened. I was halfway up the side of one gorge, hopelessly tangled in leatherwood, suspended out over a vertical drop when the branch, upon which I had fully committed my entire weight and balance, snapped. Helpless, I was falling.

It's remarkable how much thinking can be done in the short time of free falling, how many conversations are entertained, how many scenarios are reviewed. I fully expected at any moment to feel my bones snap and crunch inside me and then feel the nausea sweep through. Within a few seconds I might be in incredible pain, or total blackness. There seemed no way I would escape unscathed from such a long drop and there was absolutely nothing I could do.

I was surprised at how calm I was, how resigned to my fate I seemed to be as I dropped – perhaps because at last matters had been taken out of my hands. Nothing I did from this point on was going to affect the outcome. What would be would be, and fighting it was futile. Not having slept for two days I was so tired it no longer mattered. Since I wasn't talking to The Source I didn't even mutter a quiet prayer or ask for rescue. I just knew this was it.

I only fell for a few seconds before I hit the first obstacle. I smacked into a branch

You always hurt the one you love. . . yourself.

Dennis Potter

Almost all our faults are more pardonable than the methods we think up to hide them.

Anon

with my forehead and this tipped the rest of my body, still under the effect of gravity, downward until miraculously all of me was caught in a collection of other branches below. I was dazed and slightly incredulous that I hadn't broken anything. Apart from the very sore bump on my head there didn't seem to be any serious damage. I wasn't in any other pain.

Amazingly I had survived quite intact. I didn't deserve to. I had no reason to be okay, yet I had been spared. Miracle or luck? God's hand or fate? I don't know but what was interesting was the song now playing in my head – an old pop tune by The Platters, *The Great Pretender.*

I smiled as it finally dawned on me. I'd sat in a café two years before and played that song on a juke box over and over. It must have really irked everyone else in the café, but I was obsessed by it. I didn't know why I was playing it for I had lost no great love, I wasn't pretending she was still around, why on earth was I so drawn to this song? I was puzzled, quite perplexed. Why was it haunting me so? At the time I let it go, simply enjoying it for the great old rock-and-roll song it was. Now I knew. It had been a gentle reminder I was pretending God was still around whereas I'd actually shut the Divine out of my life.

Here too, while we both knew that what we both wanted was to be back in love, together again, I persisted in pretending I was doing okay on my own. God couldn't connect with me and a true relationship was not possible.

Humiliation is the beginning of sanctification.

John Donne

Unfortunately, consumed by my panic and ashamed by my lack of trust, I still kept the spiritual at arm's length. The fall wasn't enough for me to reinstate diplomatic relations. I received it as a type of ambassadorial message and filed it away for future reference, meanwhile continuing on with my journey, albeit a bit more carefully.

Eventually, around mid-afternoon, I reached the lower valley rendezvous point, rigged my radio aerial, and phoned base. My big toes seemed to have gone very white at the ends, as if they'd had popped blisters. We all decided that I should get medical attention. I was still a one- or two-day walk from the nearest road, so I agreed to pay for a helicopter out.

An hour or so later I was flying. It was a hairy ride in the 80-knot winds, but I hardly noticed, I wasn't really there. It was all happening too fast, as if I was in some sort of cocooned dream or watching a movie about myself. I was detached and remote, quite

The weakness of a soul is proportionate to the number of truths that must be kept from it.

Eric Hoffer

unconnected to what was going on around me. I certainly couldn't face God, so I drifted and let events take their course. We landed at the hospital and half an hour later I was discharged.

Yes, I had been frostbitten, but there was nothing the medical staff could do. It was just a matter of wait and see what would happen. My toes would either get better or they would deteriorate. Great, that's exactly what I'd been told up the mountain by someone who didn't have a medical degree! When pressed, the doctor did think it was a good idea I'd come out of the environment, as another freezing may have done more permanent damage.[1] *C'est la vie.*

I rang the friend who had dropped me off 37 days before. After he picked me up we stopped at the supermarket to buy some groceries. As I entered the store I was overwhelmed by the deluge of sensations – stimulation overload. So many dazzling colors, so much noise, such quantities of food, so much of everything! My perceptive processes almost jammed with the input, as did my estimation of time. The first five hours I spent back in civilization felt like five days,

[1] For an explanation of why I was predisposed toward frostbite, see Appendix 2.

for that's how long it would have taken to receive a similar amount of external stimulation on the mountain. So much was coming at me, so much to register, consider and process, so much busy-ness! In contrast, the five weeks I'd spent in the mountains now seemed like five days.

That night I had my first bath in five weeks and my first long conversation in three. I put off thinking about not completing the whole 40 days and 40 nights. I wasn't afraid, I didn't think I'd failed, I just didn't know and I needed to gather a bit more momentum before I confronted it. I still hadn't plugged into the spiritual realms, as I was apprehensive about what I might find.

I needn't have worried as forces infinitely bigger than my petty guilt processes were in charge.

Well before dawn the next morning I woke up between clean sheets to this.

In the early morning before it was light He took himself off to a quiet place to pray.

So this was it. Time to go and face the music. Would I have to do it all again perhaps? Would the whole sorry saga be played over and over to show me my mistakes, to point out where I went wrong? By flashlight I walked through the drizzle to huddle in the

To find the point where hypothesis and fact meet; the delicate equilibrium between dream and reality; the place where fantasy and earthly things are metamorphosed into a work of art; the hour when faith in the future becomes knowledge of the past; to lay down one's power for others in need; to shake off the old ordeal and get ready for the new; to question, knowing that never can the full answer be found; to accept uncertainties quietly, even our incomplete knowledge of God; this is what man's journey is about, I think.

Lillian Smith

When Christ said: "I was hungry and you fed me," he didn't mean only the hunger for bread and for food; he also meant the hunger to be loved. Jesus himself experienced this loneliness. He came amongst his own and his own received him not, and it hurt him then and it has kept on hurting him. The same hunger, the same loneliness, the same having no one to be accepted by and to be loved and wanted by. Every human being in that case resembles Christ in his loneliness; and that is the hardest part, that's real hunger.

Mother Teresa

Whatever God does, the first outburst is compassion.

Meister Eckhart

woodshed. There, perched on a wooden chopping block, I looked out, toward the grey, still rain-draped hills and instantly

Lord I come to you
the weaknesses I see in me
Will be stripped away
by the power of your love

© Geoff Bullock *"The Power of Your Love"* 1992

I cried and cried and cried. What unconditional love this was! Not a word of condemnation or reproach, no hint of my letting the side down, not even a "Well, that wasn't one of your better moments was it" sort of thing. God wanted nothing else but to give me love. Pure unadulterated love. My Own Ones couldn't even remember what it was I had or hadn't done. It meant nothing to Them. All They wanted was to love me and Their only sadness was that for some inexplicable reason I had chosen not to receive it. I was still playing by my rules and I had been shown yet again that The Source's economy is completely different from the way I and the rest of the world operate. There is no tit for tat, no "you do this and you'll earn that," it is all free. I am the only impediment to receiving it.

This was beyond anything I had ever experienced. It was an economy and way of operating that was a totally foreign country to me, a country where no one spoke my language; yet when I turned up I was welcomed and celebrated as if I were a member of their royal family coming home to reclaim my inheritance. Just turning up was enough for them. All that was required of me was to accept or reject the benefits that were legally mine by birth. There were no strings attached, no debt owed, nothing to do but to take and enjoy all that was the family's, and now mine, forever.

I stood up and walked out of the woodshed, down the driveway, past paddocks of still slumbering cattle and sheep, and wandered along the road toward where I had entered the mountains more than five weeks before. As I strolled along the tune of one of my favorite Bette Midler songs came to mind.

They sang to me that I was Their hero, that I was just what They'd always hoped and prayed I would be, that everything I'd done had pleased them, that I was indeed, the wind beneath their wings.

But in the eyes of God, the infinite spirit, all the millions that have lived and now live do not make a crowd, He only sees each individual.

Søren Kierkegaard

TWENTY-TWO

Good Luck, Bad Luck

On what would have been the 40th night of
my journey, the whole of New Zealand was
struck by the worst storm so far that year. A
bitterly cold blizzard straight from Antarc-
tica dumped snow and ice over the entire
country, blocking roads and completely
blanketing the mountain ranges where I
had been. The next morning I drove to the
road end where I would have re-emerged
on day 41. Looking out through the steamy
car window at the snowflakes still falling, it
looked very miserable indeed.

*An humble knowledge
of one's self is a surer
road to God than a
deep searching of the
sciences.*

Thomas à Kempis

"Thank God I'm not out there in that," I
muttered.

*What makes you think it would be
like this if you were still out there?*

Dare I believe? Dare I believe that natural events would be altered for me? Maybe, maybe not, but of the 37 days I was in the mountains, 27 had been fine. Usually it's the other way round, 10 or 12 fine days would be the expected norm. It had been one of the mildest autumn/early winter periods for many years. Luck? Coincidence? Providence? Who knows?

By cutting short my solitude I had time to spend with my parents. My father had suffered a mild stroke while I'd been away. This period with him and my mother was the longest I'd been with them since I'd left home 25 years before. So, were my frostnipped toes good luck or bad luck? Who knows? We are sensible to leave such conclusions to God, as one of my favorite stories by Anthony de Mello shows.

There is a story of an old Chinese farmer who had an old horse for tilling his fields. One day the horse escaped into the hills and when all the neighbors sympathized with the old man over his bad luck, the farmer replied, "Bad luck? Good luck? Who knows?"

A week later the horse returned with a herd of wild horses from the hills and this time the neighbors congratulated the farmer

Not everything that is more difficult is more meritorious.
St .Thomas Aquinas

Faith is the highest passion in a human being. Many in every generation may not come that far, but none comes further.
Søren Kierkegaard

*on his good luck. His reply was, "Good luck?
Bad luck? Who knows?" Then when the
farmer's son was attempting to break in one
of the wild horses, he fell off its back and
broke his leg. Everyone thought this very bad
luck. Not the farmer whose only reaction
was, "Bad luck? Good luck? Who knows?"*

*Some weeks later the army marched into
the village and conscripted every able-bod-
ied youth they found there. When they saw
the farmer's son with his broken leg they let
him off. Now was that, "Good luck? Bad luck?
Who knows?" Everything that seems on the
surface to be evil may be good in disguise.
And everything that seems good on the surface may really be an evil. So we are wise
when we leave it to God to decide what is
good luck and what is bad, and thank him
that all things turn out for good with those
who love him.[1]*

I had been given an intensive five-week
management training course in simplicity.
For decades I'd been conditioned to get
things done, to work more efficiently, more
profitably, to "get" experiences, education,
reputation, skills, resources, words. Yet everything I'd ever needed was right in front

*The real voyage of
discovery consists not
in seeking new
landscapes, but in
having new eyes.*

Marcel Proust

[1]   from *Unencumbered by Baggage*: Tony de Mello, *A prophet for
our times.*

of me, always had been, always would be. All I had to do was take it.

I went into the mountains with a desire to discover who I was, what I was meant to be and what my purpose in life was. To do this I attempted in my own clumsy way to let The One who is without equal be my one and only guide. Along the way I discovered a little bit of how The Source works, what it really is, and how I am seen. In looking for my true colors, I glimpsed God's.

My soul journey didn't start and end on the mountain. It's been ongoing for years and is still going on. But up there, uncluttered by events, other people, and with my defenses down, God stood revealed in ways I'd never experienced before.

Some of what happened made sense, some didn't, some still doesn't. I'm grateful for this because it reduces the separation between "up there" and "down here." However, one thing that has become clear is that I can now better assess my patterns of behavior and decide which ones are in response to other people or events.

Looking back I can see that just to stay healthy for 37 days on less than subsistence rations, much of the time in subzero temperatures, was a miracle in itself. I lost around nine kilograms in weight. Usually

The world is wonderful and beautiful and good beyond one's wildest imagination. Never, never, never could o ne conceive what love is, beforehand, never. Life can be great – quite godlike. It can be so. God be thanked I have proved it.

D. H. Lawrence

this would predispose me to many illnesses: mouth ulcers, flu, colds, maybe even pleurisy or pneumonia. I didn't succumb to any of these as I believe I was living in the most stress-free environment I've ever experienced. Never before have I felt so totally and absolutely loved. Fear, worry and anxiety, with the exception of the final few days, were not on the agenda.

Worry is a form of fear, and all forms of fear produce fatigue. A man who has learned not to feel fear will find the fatigue of daily life enormously diminished.

Betrand Russell

For me this spiritual journey ranks as the most worthwhile thing I have ever done, for my soul has been reinstated to its rightful owner. God's claim and love for me goes on. I still hear the songs placed on my heart, and I am constantly challenged to openly receive what's sent my way. I continue to stray into doing things in my own strength, but now I'm not so afraid of making mistakes. I can blunder and fail and it's all right. I think it's called boasting in your weakness. It's one of the best of the multitude of blessings I've received.

To be the best of which we are capable, our religion (or world view) must be a wholly personal one, forged entirely through the fire of our questioning and doubting in the crucible of our own experience of reality.

M. Scott Peck

Not everyone needs a wilderness experience. I'm sure others may gain in a few moments what took me five weeks. I believe, however, that to get past our theology and to really experience God, we somehow need to clear the decks – to let God get at us and us at God. How we do that is as individual as each one of us.

On the mountain I found my true home. It is with The Creator, The Source, who wants nothing more than to spoil me with blessings galore. I find it hard to believe that all God wants is to enjoy my company. And why? Simply because I am loved. So incredibly loved. Truly loved beyond comprehension by an omnipotent presence that is so vast as to be almost insensible.

This love is showered on me directly and from others who I now know also love me outrageously. All I have to do is receive it. I know this is God's desire for each of us. My prayer is that through this preposterous love for me, others may somehow experience God. I pray this for you, knowing that as you accept it, you can't help but pass it on. Bless.

The heart of him who truly loves is a paradise on earth; he has God in himself, for God is love.

Félicité Robert de Lamennais

So sit down by the river
Watch the stream flow
Recall all the dreams
That you once used to know
Things you've forgotten
That took you away
To pastures not greener
But meaner…
Go up to the mountain
Go up to the glen
When silence will touch you
And heartbreak will mend.

I'm Tired Joey Boy © Van Morrison

TWENTY-THREE

Postcript – 12 Months Later

Many folk were intrigued to know if the experience changed me. Did it last? Was I completely and irrevocably transformed or was this just one of those mountain-top experiences that's all but lost? Well, yes and no. Everything's the same but everything's different.

Much to Christine's relief my first words to her when I returned were, "Don't change a thing, everything's perfect the way it is!" All along, her misgivings about the trip had not been so much for my physical safety, but that I'd return so altered that life as we knew it would be over. Friends and relatives were also relieved to find I was still me, just more so.

The best way to know God is to love many things.

Vincent van Gogh

At first I was so full of love for every-one it was a bit embarrassing for them! It was as if a long-lost love button deep within me was now on an external console ready to be triggered by any passing word, scene, or thought. It was the same as on the mountain; my emotions had their governor off, there were fewer self-protect mechanisms in place. I was open and more vulnerable, spontaneous and gushy. I would weep with joy, express affection readily. Frequently I'd find myself just sitting and watching the beautiful world and lovely family I was part of.

In the faces of men and women I see God.

Walt Whitman

At first I was relatively unguarded with others, but over time this diminished as candor of that kind is not always welcome. My increased frankness also produced friction between Christine and myself, but we soon re-adjusted to each other, further deepening our love/marriage. It's never been better.

When I spoke about my experiences to individuals or groups I'd sometimes touch on a memory and would once again become caught up in the awe of it all. Taken unawares like this I'd weep as a gush of wonder gripped me. I couldn't predict at what point of the discourse this would occur – it just happened.

After I finished talking there was often a period of complete silence. No comments, nothing. At first this unnerved me – had I offended someone? Had they been listening? There were few of the usual questions one gets at the end of a talk or during a conversation. What I said seemed to be enough. When it began to happen on a regular basis I realized that somehow, something much bigger than my words was touching others in a very real way.

Even so, I felt frustrated that I wasn't communicating the true essence. I'd leave each conversation aware there was so much left unsaid, so much more to tell, and I had to tell it. I would have exploded if I couldn't! So I began to write.

I wrote and re-wrote until satisfied I had an honest account of how it really was. While writing I more or less dropped out as I didn't want other influences to intrude. I avoided television and films, read few books, newspapers or magazines, and advised friends I'd not be calling for a while.

When I finally resurfaced months later, I was keen to find out how many others might have had similar experiences. My search led me to some fascinating material. Although few had embarked upon a journey of solitude like mine, there were many

God enters by a private door into every individual.

Ralph Waldo Emerson

Men talk of "finding God," but no wonder it is difficult; He is hidden in that darkest hiding-place, your heart. You yourself are a part of Him.

Christopher Morley

whose experience of the "inner voice" or "otherness" was strikingly similar. Indeed, deeply moving, profoundly spiritual moments are quite widespread among ordinary, everyday people in Western countries. Some surveys have revealed that up to two-thirds of the population, including a significant proportion of those describing themselves as agnostic or atheist, claim to have had an experience of "God." My delight in finding out I wasn't alone or some sort of religious nut, was tempered with puzzlement: if God is being experienced so intimately by so many, how come it's such a secret? This is now a subject I'm passionately pursuing.

However, mingled with the pleasure of researching and writing was the fear of not earning enough money to keep the family going. This fear constantly dogged me. My faith in providence was fragile on the mountain; it's even more shaky in the mainstream of life. I fluctuated from inspired, optimistic confidence when payments came in, to dispirited despair when we found it necessary to increase the mortgage. As with my frostnipped toes, the case for the prosecution was as loud as the case for the defense.

If you don't get work soon you'll go broke.

Each of us has at least once in his life experienced the momentous reality of God.

Joshua Heschel

When have you ever gone without?
What a fool to waste your time writ-
ing. That's no way to pay your bills.
What you're doing is enough.

Eventually, as on the mountain, what was
needed – reassurance, comfort, sustenance,
insight – was inevitably provided, just in
time. Again and again what I saw as frustrating obstacles would often turn out to be
divine delays. I'm still a slow learner in matters of trusting God.

One thing has definitely changed. Although fear at times grips me, it doesn't de-
rail me into total panic like it used to. There's
an ember now buried deep inside that continues to quietly glow. I don't consciously
have to reach for it, I'm just aware of its presence. This gentle "knowing" has resulted in
letting go of a lot of the individual responsibility I've always felt. I used to believe that
if I didn't work hard, if I didn't raise my children right, then it would all go off the rails.
Now I don't feel so personally liable for everything that goes right or wrong. I'm freer
to make mistakes. Freer to be who I really
am rather than who I think I have to be.

In this regard the world has lost some
of its hold on me. Although I'm still anxious
and want to please people, there's now an
underlying sense that these things don't

God will forgive me;
it is His trade.
Heinrich Heine

With some people
solitariness is an
escape not from
others but from
themselves. For
they see in the eyes
of others only
a reflection
of themselves.
Eric Hoffer

matter so much anymore. My life's only 70 to 80 odd years in the billion-year spectrum; my great-great-grandchildren will one day be here, and I now realize I'm only a small, but very cherished, part of something much bigger.

At work and surrounded by the busyness of everyday life, it's difficult to move in the gentle rhythms of grace. The sheer volume of sensory input often crowds out the inner voice, but that doesn't mean it's disappeared, rather it's just switched channels. I'm now learning to listen to outer voices and to discern from them what the inner voice is saying. It's more complicated than when alone, but solitude has shown me the patterns to look for.

Most evenings I walk my dog to a high rocky lookout point about a kilometer from my back door. There we sit and gaze out over the beautiful bushland valleys to the far-off mountains. Once in a while we stay for an hour or so, but usually it's only a few minutes – I to wonder and muse, sometimes to worry; she to ponder bones to chew or smells to sniff. Sometimes we watch a sunset, sometimes it's the moon and the stars.

In summer, the heat evaporating the eucalyptus oil from the trees produces a dense haze turning the distant mountains

Two men please God – who serves Him with all his heart because he knows Him; who seeks Him with all his heart because he knows Him not.

Nikita Ivanovich Panin

blue. In winter the clear air yields a continual smorgasbord of stunning sunsets. Each time we take the same route, the same actions take place between dog and human: I speak the same words; she puts her head under my arm for a cuddle. We always take the same path home.

Never before have I done anything so repetitive for so long, with no thought of how to make it more interesting, challenging, rewarding, or different. In these moments I need no more than what is happening and have no desire to change it in any way.

There is a time for everything and a season for every activity under heaven.

Ecclesiastes

When we arrive home I return the dog to her run, pour biscuits into her bowl, and give her one final pat. Then, as I slowly walk up the path back to the house, I don't even notice how blissfully unaware I am of anything missing or lacking. All is complete. I think it's called contentment.

How Do I Know Who's Talking in There?

In tuning in to my inner voice I didn't audibly hear "voices, "rather I just monitored the random unconnected images, notions and thoughts that floated through my head. Becoming aware of them I'd check them out using the following criteria. It's by no means a complete list, but for me it was an essential tool for discernment.

I considered my random unconnected thoughts from God if they were:

- Peaceful
- Consistent
- Loving
- Patient
- Uplifting
- Instructive

- Comforting
- Clear
- Kind
- Welcoming of scrutiny
- Seldom needing to be responded to in a hurry.

I put them down as coming from myself rather than the spiritual realms if they:

- Were a logical processed outcome of things I'd learned or deduced
- Appealed to my ego
- Varied all the time depending on the information I'd received
- Would eventually make me look good in front of others.

However, if the spontaneous thoughts were along these lines:

- An accusation
- Confusing
- Promoted fear and panic
- Rejected scrutiny
- Produced guilt
- Created anxiety and generally unsettled me
- Were pushy, urgent, wanting to be done in a hurry – a driving compulsion to "do it now,"

I ascribed them to the spiritual realms, but not the heavenly ones.

I'm human. I often got it wrong, but this

was part of the exercise: to better discern where the messages were coming from before I acted on them. They didn't only occur when I was still. I could be walking, half asleep, deeply engrossed in something, or quite distracted and then slowly or suddenly become aware of a picture, phrase, scene, song lyric, snatch of conversation that seemed lodged uppermost in my consciousness.

Back in civilization, the spiritual realm sometimes becomes clear to me through "coincidences," remarkable synchronicity, the same thought or idea coming from a variety of unrelated sources. Occasionally I simply get a deep intuitive sense that a particular course of action is right, though on the surface it might appear quite illogical. It was such a perception that took me to the mountains.

I didn't do this alone. I constantly asked for help and guidance so that I could clearly discern The Voice. I also tried to judge my spiritual progress not by how I felt, but by how I acted.

Details On Frosbite

Frostbite is a cold burn. Like hot burns there are varying degrees of it. I had first degree, the mildest. My toes were frozen and the nerves in them killed off. Full recovery is quite usual and takes from one to six months. So why, with all my good equipment, was I frostbitten?

Our bodies have an amazing built-in regulatory system to cope with cold. It's all based around keeping our central core temperature warm. Our extremities lose the body's heat quickest of all, so in prolonged cold conditions the body reduces to a minimum the heat supply to these outer regions. It does this by thickening the blood. (Thick blood is hard to pump into the small capillaries that feed the fingers, nose and toes.) The blood is made thicker by shedding excess water, which is why you urinate quite profusely when cold.

The blood-thickening process means that whenever you're in extreme cold for any length of time, without access to external warmth, your body dehydrates. Even though you feel fine, you have to make a conscious effort to avoid dehydration by drinking more, which is quite difficult as you're not in the least bit thirsty.

I was on the mountain tops for four weeks. Most of the time there was a sprinkling of snow, and this, combined with the wind, probably kept the temperatures to zero Celsius and often well below. The last week it got considerably colder with 40 to 60 centimeters of snow lying around. I noticed I urinated often, which seemed strange as I wasn't drinking all that much. My inner voice kept inviting me to "Have a cuppa." At the time I thought it was a boredom reducing exercise, but I now see it differently. My stools were also extremely hard and very difficult to pass, another symptom of dehydration. At the time I just put it down to my reduced diet. The below subsistence level rations also meant my body didn't have food to burn to produce its own heat. Whatever heat produced was retained in my body core, further predisposing my extremities to frostbite. With my already thickened blood, snow and ice I'd normally shuffle through with no ill effects now had the capacity to frostnip my toes.

As it turned out, my toes took three months to fully regain feeling and to return to normal. I panicked on the mountain because I had no knowledge of frostbite, its levels of severity, and what you should or shouldn't do. I now know it would have been okay to stay on and walk out when the 40 days were up. However, there was a real danger that with numb toes I wouldn't have been able to tell if I injured or refroze them. The worst thing to do with frostbite is to thaw the flesh and then refreeze it. There is little to no chance of recovery for the affected limbs if you do this. On the other hand, quite severe frostbite – black bits and all – is not always a disaster and almost full recovery is expected if you look after the damage properly.